COVID-U
BUSINESS LESSONS
FROM
A PANDEMIC

COVID-U
BUSINESS LESSONS
FROM
A PANDEMIC

Jay Prag
Claremont Graduate University, USA

Amanda Ishak Prag

 **World Scientific**

NEW JERSEY · LONDON · SINGAPORE · BEIJING · SHANGHAI · HONG KONG · TAIPEI · CHENNAI · TOKYO

Published by

World Scientific Publishing Co. Pte. Ltd.

5 Toh Tuck Link, Singapore 596224

USA office: 27 Warren Street, Suite 401-402, Hackensack, NJ 07601

UK office: 57 Shelton Street, Covent Garden, London WC2H 9HE

Library of Congress Control Number: 2022948961

British Library Cataloguing-in-Publication Data
A catalogue record for this book is available from the British Library.

COVID-U
Business Lessons from a Pandemic

ISBN 978-981-126-772-7 (hardcover)
ISBN 978-981-126-773-4 (ebook for institutions)
ISBN 978-981-126-774-1 (ebook for individuals)

For any available supplementary material, please visit
https://www.worldscientific.com/worldscibooks/10.1142/13181#t=suppl

Desk Editor: Ong Shi Min Nicole

Typeset by Stallion Press
Email: enquiries@stallionpress.com

Printed in Singapore

Contents

Acknowledgments

COVID-19 forever changed the lives of millions of people around the world. As much as this book tries to take a positivist look at negative events, we acknowledge that this writing does not address the suffering encountered by those affected by the pandemic. We are not thankful for the opportunity to explore such events. We wish the topic of this book had never emerged.

As academics, we are aware that we think for a living. That's it. So, our sincerest thanks go out to everyone who helped facilitate this writing, especially Samir and Frieda Ishak, without whom this book would never have been possible. We are also grateful to the many colleagues who reviewed our work: your dedication to research and truth has been invaluable to this process. We would also like to thank Ong Shi Min Nicole and all of the people at World Scientific Publishing who helped to bring this book to fruition.

Our daughter, Julianna, was three months old when the world shut down in early 2020. By some counts, that makes her a Pandemic Baby (maybe). Her resilience inspires us every day. She went down "the big red slide" at the playground the other day. That's what matters. This book doesn't. And, ultimately, we acknowledge that.

About the Authors

Jay Prag is a Clinical Full Professor of Economics and Finance at the Peter F. Drucker and Masotoshi Ito School of Management at Claremont Graduate University, where he has been teaching since 1986. He holds a PhD in Economics from the University of Rochester and a Bachelor of Business Administration from the University of Florida. Jay has authored several economics texts, including *Microeconomic Essentials* (MIT Press). He has also co-authored *Macroeconomic Essentials* (MIT Press) with Peter Kennedy, and *Financial Management for Executives* with James Wallace (Cambridge Business Press).

Amanda Ishak Prag earned a PhD in Management from the University of California, Riverside, where she taught the capstone undergraduate course Competitive and Strategic Analysis. She also holds an MBA from Claremont Graduate University and a Bachelor of Economics and a Bachelor of Public Relations from the University of Southern California. Amanda is Director of Marketing for one of the largest architecture and engineering firms in the United States. She works with a variety of clients to develop strategic communication, recruiting, and project management plans.

Amanda and Jay reside in sunny and overpriced Southern California with their daughter, Julianna, and their two dogs, Doc Brown and Marty.

Prologue

Welcome to Covid University, where everyone is admitted, and the program never ends.

From every angle, the world has faced unprecedented change over the past two years. Academics will be dissecting the nuance of the Covid Crisis for decades to come (this is, after all, what they do best). For all the promises of research and data, we must understand that the full impact of the pandemic on everything — from child development and college football seasons to healthcare breakthroughs and the future of the film industry — will not be known for a generation at least. Of course, the "new normal," that horrible cliché, has yet to be defined. At this point, the best we can hope for is a reflection on some of the immediate changes that occurred and ask, perhaps rhetorically, whether we may ever return to the old normal.

This book focuses on the business lessons we have learned *so far* since the saga began in early 2020. Although we are circuiting key issues related to economic solvency, growth, and income, we do not suggest that this narrative comes close to articulating anything important. We are talking about Pelotons and AMC theaters, not lifesaving therapies and life-after-death. So, please excuse a bit of sarcasm and a lot of flippancy in the following pages. We respect the business world; we work, live, and play in it. But it is not as important as the everyday struggles of those truly facing this pandemic. We do not mean to make light of the pain Covid has caused millions, only to examine some of the specific changes observed in this new world.

Chapter 1: Introduction: Never Waste a Good Pandemic

The Covid pandemic is an ongoing, large-scale natural experiment producing billions of data points every day. The first lesson is to never waste an opportunity to learn from a challenge. With respect for what has been lost, our first chapter establishes the lens through which all lessons could emerge.

Chapter 2: Pandora's Box

Here comes the horde(r). Many of the adaptations companies made to existing products and services had to be quick, leaving little time for a beta test. This worked well in most cases, but was it all good news? In Chapter 2, we examine some of the underpinnings of change in consumer and producer preferences and how businesses may have to revisit decisions made early in the pandemic.

Chapter 3: Competitive Advantage, Meet Covid

Across B-to-B, B-to-C, and other aptly lettered business sectors, Covid was a game changer. With a paradigm shift (there, we said it) in the competitive environment, businesses are scrambling to understand where their *real* competitive advantage is — or whether they have one at all.

Chapter 4: High Noon: Corporate Culture

How much of a difference did that pool table make in the break room? Does your company's matrix organizational structure have you reporting to five people? Do your employees *really* like working (for you)? This chapter looks at the first (and ongoing) aspect of business affected by Covid, corporate culture, from both an employer and employee perspective.

Chapter 5: Office Lost

You (or your employees) can work from home now. Yay or nay? Getting the IT figured out was just the first step. Productivity is up or down depending on the industry. People are still leaving the labor market, but not in the places (or for the reasons) we expect. What did it truly mean to "lose" the office environment, and what does it mean now that some companies are trying to get it back?

Chapter 6: Lucky or Good?

There are clear winners, but how sustainable is their success? Chapter 6 examines products and services that may just be fleeting economies of scale, looking at companies that were able to take advantage of short-term trends but may not have an established foundation for long-term success.

Chapter 7: Right Place, Right Time

On the other hand, the pandemic helped some industries really get going. Chapter 7 looks at firms whose success stories might be here to last, especially those whose long-term strategies found a place during the pandemic. Unlike lucky firms, companies in the right place at the right time might see enduring success even as the pandemic recedes.

Chapter 8: If Your Home Is Your Castle, Is It Time to Re-moat?

So, you're working from home, and it's working. Do you need to re-moat? This chapter looks at some of the sustainable benefit drivers for the segment of the work force that can work at home indefinitely. For many industries, Covid indisputably changed the definitions of compensation, mobility, and flexibility, and we look at the impacts this shift may have on the businesses that employ workforce with changing preferences.

Chapter 9: Marketing with a Mask

The pandemic changed marketing forever. This was perhaps the first "industry" to see real change, and with the prevalence of data and the need for immediate results, it is also the easiest to dissect. In this chapter, we look at how the pandemic affected marketing from both a producer and consumer perspective and suggest ways this may impact the launch of new products and services in the future.

Epilogue: Hello From the Other Side

We all have at-home gym equipment and big screens now. What's next? This chapter examines some of the ongoing evolutions — and remaining questions — for the trajectory of Covid and its effects on the business environment.

In each chapter, we include an overview of the topic and a breakdown of major issues, plus:

- *Concept Reviews*, to help explain some of the economics that drive these issues.
- *Mini Case Studies*, to illustrate the concepts in the real world.
- *Discussion Questions*, to apply the concepts to other contexts and environments. We have also provided guiding notes to the questions at the end of the book.

As the world adapts to ongoing crises and the sands continue to shift beneath us, we know the Covid pandemic is one piece of the human experience in our time. Still, we hope the discussions provided in this book provide another layer of understanding of the complexities of strategic change. Thank you for reading, and welcome to Covid U.

April 2022

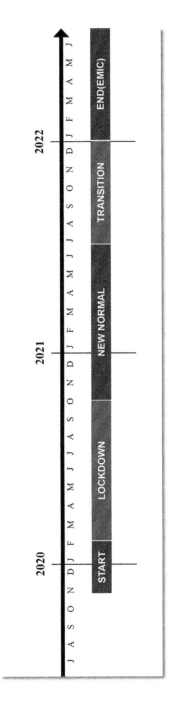

COVID-19 Pandemic: Definition of Phases

COVID-19 Pandemic: Definition of Phases

Start: *November 2019–February 2020. At the start of the COVID-19 pandemic, information was coming in, but it had not yet coalesced into a clear picture. While the world was increasingly aware of COVID-19 and the implications of widespread disease, no actions had yet been taken on a grand scale.*

Lockdown: *March 2020–September 2020. As coverage of the virus continued to dominate news feeds, municipalities across the country and across the world began enacting policies to limit exposure. These policies ranged from mask requirements to all-out curfews and daily lockdowns. Although this phase lasted through Fall of 2020, it was acute, with most lockdowns taking effect in the 30 days between March 15 and April 14, 2022. From that time, regulations were adjusted for the next six months.*

New Normal: *October 2020–June 2021. As variants continue to dominate headlines, businesses that have been open and functioning under lockdowns continue operations and businesses that were slowed or stopped begin to open. Virtual and remote work continues where possible. Mask mandates, indoor gathering limitations, and other regulations remain in place. Vaccine programs ramp up, including availability of the first boosters.*

Transition: *July 2021–December 2021. Omicron variant dominates headlines and vaccine booster programs ramp up. Virtual and remote work capabilities begin to wane. In-person instruction for primary and secondary education, as well as higher education, begins to return. Significant differences in regulation can be seen between different cities within a single state/region. Retail cycles return to normal for the 2021 Holiday season. Economists begin coining the term The Great Resignation.*

End(emic): *January 2022–Present. Lockdowns around the world continue as needed but are dependent on local regulatory need. In-person activities resume in earnest. Mask mandates are repealed nationwide.*

1

Introduction: Never Waste a Good Pandemic

"Those who cannot remember the past are condemned to repeat it."
— *George Santayana, Philosopher*

Business academics need experiments — opportunities and events that allow us to vet our theories, approaches, and concepts. You can't test the veracity of any proposition unless you experience it in real-world conditions, and experiments are all about testing something in a changing environment. The emphasis is on "changing". Baseball players are never considered great hitters if they are only capable of hitting straight fastballs. A baseball player must be able to hit curveballs, changeups (slower pitches), and every other pitch to be considered truly great. A theory must hold true in a variety of circumstances to be valid.

The *real* test of a theory doesn't happen in a lab, under strict controls. It happens when we observe it under the conditions of a natural experiment — like the Covid pandemic. The naturally occurring events over the past two years give us an ability to look at all sides of a regime shift: consumers and producers, labor and employers, B-to-B, B-to-C, commodities, resources, strategic plans, and everything in between. Natural experiments used to be considered the last, almost negligible step in academia (who cares about the real world when "studies have shown…"), but they have gained favor in recent years. Interestingly, the 2021 Nobel Prize in economics was awarded to three economists who showed the usefulness of these natural experiments. True, natural experiments like the pandemic are uncontrolled, but that does not mean we cannot learn from them. On the contrary, with the right amount of data availability and the ability to process it, we can learn a great deal.

It is true that we don't usually see natural experiments as dramatic and far-reaching as COVID-19 and the economic shock that this pandemic brought forth. Between government shut-downs, fast-tracked vaccines, mask mandates, and the overall uncertainty that Covid caused, every business in the US was impacted by ongoing shockwaves. This will go down in history as a major inflection point in the global economy; a shift in trends the likes of which we rarely see. Very few individuals can say they haven't been affected by the shifting sands, and if the needs of the people change, business must follow.

As humans, and as academics, we have a golden opportunity to observe reactions and responses to all things Covid. Those who teach in business schools should look at all our areas of study — economics, strategy, marketing, leadership, organizational behavior, finance, etc. — and ask the hard questions about what we teach and how useful it is in a redefined environment. But, even those who teach outside a classroom as leaders, managers, mentors, owners, breadwinners, and parents are looking at a brave new world of pandemic-inspired lessons.

So, let's go to COVID U: the business school that looks across all disciplines in a Covid and post-Covid world and asks what did we learn and where will this end up?

Why Business?

When we refer to business, we do not take a calculated, abstract definition of the term. Business is people. It's a human, or a group of humans, trying to work with another group of humans. Put a few people together in a household, and maybe it's a family. People from different families working together: a company. If the groups get large enough, we call it an industry. But these are just bigger and bigger groups of humans. People.

People have preferences and perceptions. People have needs, wants, and biases. People's opinions matter to other people, and their behavior affects the ability of other people to live their lives. People shop in stores stocked and staffed by people. These same people saw their worlds come to a grinding halt — or get thrown into chaos — around the same time in early 2020.

People comprise businesses.

People.

Now, we know some businesses were stricken down by the pandemic, and some were saved. Some businesses were lucky in the first few rounds, but we're not sure about future change. Covid accelerated the demise of some businesses that were already on their way out while buoying others for a while. And our definitions of labor markets, productivity, employee motivation, and the nature of "work" in the post-Covid world is still being sorted out. This is a lot to work out for a lot of people.

IF they are still around, all open businesses have survived a major economic and social shock. Congratulations are in order. A lot of companies, veterans that defined the early years of their industries, did not survive. The pandemic took us both forward (Carvana) and backward (telecommuting), through permanent (homebuying) and temporary (maybe I'll wear pants again someday) change. From these stories, let's see what firms have learned and what new lessons in business they can teach all of us in the business education world.

Concept Review: Data

Aside from the fact that the word 'data' is plural and thus in need of verbs that are for plural nouns, people usually have a pretty concrete idea of what they think data means. It's numbers. When you collect data, you look at prices or wages or sales or the sort of stuff that's found in census data.

But wait, census data has a lot of things in it including descriptive things like gender. And that's a good thing to realize. Data can be lots of things. They can, indeed, be formal like numbers. These data are the ones that we often see analyzed with statistics or what's sometimes called econometrics. Of course, how the data can be accurately analyzed depends on things like how random the data is (oops, I mean are), and whether the data are describing something that occurred over time or something that occurred across the population.

We're used to hearing the results of data-based studies in headlines like, "Sixty-five percent of the population believe in UFOs," or "inflation is rising at the fastest pace in forty years."

There's a credibility that people feel when they hear something "supported" by formal, numerical data even though no data driven study is ever perfect. Polls are taken to predict population results. A small set of timeseries data is often used to support a broad claim. So, we want to allow that numbers are one form of data; we also want to smile understandingly when we hear the Mark Twain quip "Lies, damns lies, and statistics."

There's another type of data out there, well-known, and well-accepted by researchers and the like: qualitative data. As opposed to the earlier described quantitative data, qualitative data include things like interviews, observations, and other ways of learning things. As with quantitative data collection, the researcher should be careful and precise. You don't want to collect all of your data from one source if you're trying to make a general statement. And in collecting qualitative data from a variety of sources you need to be consistent and terse. The analogy of quantitative data is useful here. You collect the same data series every year, generated the same way, so that you can (for example) run a regression. In quantitative and qualitative data analysis, you can't compare apples to oranges. But overall, qualitative data are a useful and important source of information.

While we're on this subject, a note about our approach. This book has been developed using both kinds of data. There are numbers like stock prices, market shares, and profits and there is information gleaned from observations and interviews. Because we are still in the Covid era to a large extent, the quantitative data are less useful. We'll leave it to researchers a few years in the future to do more of that.

One final comment about this book and its origins. As we mentioned, we are discussing some of the first observations and results from a natural experiment. Sadly, this natural experiment had very serious, albeit natural, repercussions — illness and death. We chose not to write this book from the dark perspective that these repercussions represent to make it more readable. In so doing though, we are not making light of the seriousness of this pandemic.

Interesting Aside

Never waste a good pandemic is admittedly flippant, but we are not the first investigators to try to find something new and useful in a major calamity. One famous example is that of 19th century British physician John Snow. During an 1850s outbreak of cholera, Dr. Snow eschewed the popular myth that contagious diseases came from the air and, before the discovery of what we now call germs, he used maps and statistics to show that cholera was correlated with water. Specifically, it was closely related to the very polluted Thames River. Snow is sometimes called the father of *epidemiology*: the study of the spread of contagious disease. His contribution was followed closely by those of Louis Pasteur and Robert Koch, and all of this led to the understanding of modern germ theory. This concept is now widely accepted, even taken for granted, but it was connected to an observation born of necessity during a pandemic.

Another story from later in the 19th century was that of German Dr. Paul Ehrlich. Most early vaccines followed a protocol developed one hundred years earlier by British physician Edward Jenner who, upon noticing that dairy workers who had caught the relatively mild disease known as Cow Pox were "immune" from the much more dangerous disease Smallpox, suggested that a new area of study, immunology, could be developed to find out what increased the body's resistance to infection.

After working on vaccines with Emil Behring and Robert Koch based mostly on this approach, Dr. Ehrlich began working on a solution for a far more controversial disease: syphilis. But, rather than attempting to build up immunity, he searched for, and found, chemical compounds that actually killed the disease in the human body. Chemotherapy, and much of pharmacology, was the result of that approach.

Mini Case: Meta

Social media has become the chain letter of our times (you'll probably need to Google chain letter). The biggest social media platform in the world is Facebook. Founded in 2004 by (arguably) Mark Zuckerberg, Facebook has connected and reconnected billions of friends, family members, high school sweethearts, and others to each other's favorite vacation photos, news stories, grandchildren's artwork, and cat videos. But where there's that many people exercising the cliché sharing is caring, there's also going to be problems.

It's no fun if someone tells you what you can and can't share so as much as possible, Facebook wanted to be unfiltered. You can see the problems coming if you step back and think about it. Millions of people sharing unfiltered, unvetted, unsubstantiated drivel all of the time; Facebook and other social media platforms (notably Twitter) became politicized.

In the US, people associate the politicization of social media with Donald Trump and his 2016 victory over Hillary Clinton in the presidential election, but Barack Obama famously used this approach first in 2008. The social media roadmap was also used in the UK to mobilize support for Brexit and many governments have closed or limited social media platforms in order to control (read manipulate) the outcome of elections.

Not surprisingly, social media usage increased during the lockdown phase of Covid so the corporate executives at Facebook should have been happy folks. But founder Mark Zuckerberg was one of a handful of technology executives called to testify before Congress as part of what was described as an attempt to regulate or possibly break up several large tech companies.

Then, in an interesting twist, Facebook got a new name: Meta. Perhaps because their original name had become something of a lightning rod, perhaps because the business platform is, always was, all about data, Facebook became Meta, as in metadata.

If the idea behind this name change was to change the perspective that the company was too powerful and thus in need of regulation, does the switch to Meta help? Other companies famously changed their names over the years. In 1987, Datsun cars sold in the US were rebranded as Nissan (the corporate manufacturer) and in 2015 Google consolidated several subsidiaries and renamed itself Alphabet. In these and other cases, there's always a corporate strategy or marketing reason for the name change. Discuss these reasons.

Discussion Questions

1.1 Depending on your age, COVID-19 and all of the impacts that it has had on the economy and society might be the most important regime shift that you've ever experienced. Going back one century, there have been other dramatic events that changed everyone's life and left a mark on society: The Great Depression, World War II, the dawn of the nuclear age, disco, the Internet, and others of varying magnitude. How will your life and that of your friends and family "never be the same?" Specifically, think about the impact Covid has had on:

 a. Your ability to connect with others, whether friends or colleagues.

 b. The availability of resources to do your "job," your "hobbies," or your "daily life tasks."

 c. Your ability to adapt. How abrupt was the change, and where did it come from? (Hint: think mandates vs. slow adoption of technology). Does it matter?

 d. Your ability to evolve. Were all of the changes permanent? Which ones endured, and why do you think this happened?

1.2 Data regarding the effects of the pandemic continue to arrive by the minute. Are they helpful? What do we need data to become in order for them to be helpful? How do we get there?

1.3 Perhaps we could call the chapter never waste a good calamity. Investigate how Long Beach California earthquake of 1933 changed the building industry.

1.4 Investigate how the Stock Market Crash of 1929 and the Housing Bubble Crisis of 2008 led to changes in financial markets.

1.5 Discuss other calamities that you are familiar with and how they changed society.

2

Pandora's Box

"What fresh hell is this?"
— *Attributed in various forms to Dorothy Parker*

According to the ancient Greek story, Pandora's curiosity led her to open a box that had been left with her husband for safekeeping, irrevocably releasing curses on mankind. In the story, there was no way to get the evil spirits back into the box once released.

Oops.

Covid was a Pandora's Box moment for many businesses. In order to survive, businesses did things that they normally wouldn't. In some cases, they did things that they said they never would. We, as authors and professors, know this problem first-hand. High-touch colleges that focused on the classroom experience often said they were never going to go online. And then, they did. Because they had to. The choice we faced was go online or close.

But, there are two sides to every change: the business and the consumer that supports it. Students who came to our schools couldn't get the classroom experience during the time we were in lockdown, so they had to decide if they wanted to take our classes online; some did, some didn't. That was their choice, too.

And what about labor? Well, great classroom professors (cough, cough) had to learn how to teach online. (Hopefully) we made the experience a fruitful one, all things considered. A school that prided itself on the classroom experience needed to exceed expectations in this area, at least in the short term.

But, there's a problem; a Pandora's Box Problem. Even as things re-open and in-person classes are available again, we can't revert back to the old way of doing things. We simply can't say we "don't" do online classes anymore — because we did, and it worked. At best, we can only say we "won't" do it, and that's a very different message from the value proposition we had before.

The same thing happened to retailers. When the pandemic was in early phases and the retail environment became increasingly tense, stores like Target, Wal-Mart, and your neighborhood grocer accommodated people who wanted (needed) to buy products but did not want to enter busy stores. These retailers ramped up online ordering and drive-up service, showing they were ready to shop and carry your purchases out to your car for no extra charge — not even a tip. Some were better equipped than others, but with the infrastructure in place, it was certainly a convenient option. Consumers gobbled it up. However, this was not a "no-cost" option for businesses. In addition to hazard pay, they were looking at a fully built out (and maintained) online shopping infrastructure with real-time and reliable inventory tracking. They also needed to train (and protect) personnel, rent parking spaces, and on and on.

Now that the pandemic is humming along nicely and things have settled a bit, what do retailers do with the new system? Should drive-up always be a free service in the future? Can it be?

Given the new expectation of shoppers… can it *not* be? Retailers have to consider that they have already proven to the customer they can do it. Once this happens, how do they stop?

The idea that a concept has been proven to consumers is one example of the Pandora's Box problem created by the Covid pandemic. It is a reminder that services and products have a lifecycle; once they are launched, there is no guarantee they will remain forever. Under normal circumstances, a product or service may come under review when demand falls. A company asks: *should we still provide this if nobody wants it anymore?* This assumes the product or service was developed and launched under typical conditions, where it could be tested in a smaller market and then rolled out on a larger scale.

What we saw in the early stages of Covid, however, was companies developing products and services under duress. Same-day delivery and drive-up/contactless services were rolled out quickly and, arguably, quite efficiently. Under Covid circumstances, programs were rushed into production and services ramped up. Now, years on, it's time to review these wartime choices. Companies have to engage in product review in reverse: *should we still provide this if we don't want to anymore?*

Yes, evaluating demand is relevant here. Retailers should still ask "does anyone want this service anymore?" But, there are other key pieces of information they can now take into account: how much does the service cost, in terms of net transactions? Has it fundamentally changed the way people interact with the rest of our store? Yes, it saved us when nobody was willing to shop in person, but is it costing us now? How much does the infrastructure cost to maintain? Are people willing to shift shopping habits "back" to the old way of doing things? And the list goes on and on…

From a strategy standpoint, we might be tempted to feel bad for firms that have to engage in this retroactive analysis — but wait. They have a lot of data to look at. Unlike the "usual" way of testing out a new product or service, firms can see how it works in the real world in real time. Companies pay a lot of money ($billions) to marketing firms for projections and market tests on product launches that are, at best, educated guesses. Covid took away the guess by forcing companies to launch first and evaluate later. Moving forward, we will see what choices these companies make with the information they have become privy to.

So, Covid opened Pandora's Box for some companies: they adjusted their business to accommodate an emergency situation, and now they might not be able to adjust them back. That's the producer's conundrum. Let's look at the side of the consumer.

Unavailable products and services forced/allowed us to try other choices for our tried-and-true products (store-brand toilet paper, anyone?). The knowledge of those alternatives has forever changed what we can consider substitutes. We can't "un-try" what we've already tried. For some things, like home-based haircuts, this probably won't decrease the demand for professional salons in the long run. For other products with just-as-good substitutes and available store brands, like Kleenex or Lysol… it might.

Concept Review: Utility Theory

The market model is a cornerstone of economics. Simple and straightforward, it connects the production and distribution of a good (called the Supply) to the consumer's purchase and consumption decision (the Demand) by way of the good's price. Price needs to balance the cost of production on the Supply side (something we'll talk about again in Chapter 6) and the needs and wants of the consumer on the Demand side. If something shocks the Supply or Demand side (or both), we can see drastic shifts in what the model tells us.

In terms of the balancing act between Supply and Demand, Supply is relatively straightforward: both price and cost are already in dollar terms, and we can plot them easily. But Demand is harder, because measuring the consumer's choice in dollar terms is a little more complicated. That is, it's hard to put a price on how a consumer *feels*. One popular approach to this problem is Utility Theory.

Economists often model consumer choice by saying happiness (utility) comes from consuming a good, and that this happiness can be measured, at least well enough to explain what people buy. The utility model leans heavily on the observation that people don't usually consume large amounts of the same good at any one time. So, the model supposes that happiness rises as we consume more of a good, but it rises at a decreasing rate. This bears out in the real world: we tend to get tired of any one good as we consume more and more of it at any one time.

As with most models in economics, Utility Theory can be shown graphically or using calculus. We usually teach it with a simple chart, since the calculus implies that you're consuming an infinitely small additional amount of each good at a time (and, even though the math is supremely elegant, who really eats 1/8th of a donut at a time?). A table of donut utilities, for example, looks something like Table 2.1.

Table 2.1:   Diminishing marginal utility of donuts

No. of Donuts	Jollies	Marginal Utility
1	30	30
2	50	20
3	60	10
4	65	5
5	66	1

Happiness, measured in "jollies", rises with every donut shown but it rises at a decreasing rate. The increment to our happiness, called marginal utility (MU), gets smaller as I consume more donuts at any one time. Assuming all goods have a similar chart, and goods cost money (suppose the price of donuts is $1), consumers will allocate income — specifically, their next dollar — to maximize their jollies. You don't typically spend the additional dollar on a fifth (or probably even fourth) donut. Why? Because, by the time you've already eaten that many donuts, there are other goods (like, maybe, a soda?) that will give you more happiness for that additional dollar.

Utility Theory explains, in part, the observed inverse relationship between price and quantity demanded by the consumer. As the price of a good falls, a consumer will allocate more income to that good because it becomes a cheaper source of jollies. It's an easy model to nitpick into uselessness (indeed, many economists have made an entire career doing this), but it is also easy to see Utility Theory at work in the real world.

Utility Theory has a few key takeaways.

First, if consumers are being sensible, they will usually make a choice that fits their utility choices. We know that children and drug addicts do not make sensible choices, and we can explain that with a slight tweak of the model: their jollies are skewed to support their choices, unique to their circumstances. We can also use this theory to explain the existence of marketing: people need to be informed to know the jollies that could come from a good, and if you can convince people their jollies will be higher with your product, you win. Within marketing, we can see how brand names help explain utility: they give consumers a familiar set of expectations for a particular good. They can rely on the brand as a consistent source of a level of jollies.

The idea that consumers *choose* between related goods is the key point here. Economists assume (of course) that consumers choose where to pay their additional dollar <u>knowing about all other choices</u>. Some alternative uses of that dollar *augment* the jollies of your current choice (coffee and donuts might give you more jollies than donuts alone). These are called <u>complements</u>. Other goods that give you jollies in the same or similar way (croissants or muffins instead of donuts) are called *substitutes*.

Goods with lots of substitutes will have a big change in quantity demanded when their price changes. There are many ways to get jollies from consuming fruit, and there are a lot of fruits, so we don't buy as many apples when their price increases relative to other fruits. We can buy oranges or pears or watermelon or berries or, or, or… When the price of apples goes up, we can easily substitute it because we know about all the other fruits out there.

So, knowledge of substitutes is a big part of the demand for any good. Covid dramatically changed that for a lot of goods. We now know about a *lot* more options for things that we used to think were unique. To be fair, the information available from the internet, social media, and other modern sources was in place some time ago, but Covid and subsequent lockdowns with little-to-no warning pushed our knowledge about substitutes into hyperdrive. Store brand toilet paper was the only type available. When that went away, bidets became all the rage. Some people have switched brands forever. Some will never go back to toilet paper altogether. (We will discuss these things again in Chapter 9.)

Despite all the YouTube videos, you've probably realized that the trained professionals at Supercuts do a better job of coiffing you than your significant other, your offspring, or you yourself. That's true of pedicures, waxes, massages, and many other services, too.

Beyond the quality, we've also learned that there's a social aspect to the service sector. You can gossip with your stylist, and you can share photos of your kids with your bartender. We learned that there are many "bartenders" in our society with whom we share our stories. It's not just about getting a mixed drink, it's about the experience. "Substitutes" for experiential industries like these are therefore temporary — you can put them back in the box even though you know they exist. Eventually, the risk–return ratio of engaging with service providers decreases and people re-engage with these professions in a real, sustainable way.

But other experiential businesses, like high-end restaurants, might have a tougher time reclaiming lost customers. Often very expensive, many of these restaurants closed during the pandemic, and thus lost their market forever. These businesses banked on a regular clientele and time-honored, hard-to-get ratings and reputations. Once closed, high-end restaurants will have to start over. In an industry where 9 of every 10 new restaurants fails in the first year *usually*, this can be daunting. There are a lot of substitutes for expensive dining, even with a great experience attached. With high start-up costs, this is one industry that will find it harder to escape Pandora's Box.

Economics has largely ignored Pandora's Box as a problem, in that they often assume we know a lot more than we do about substitutes and tradeoffs. The pandemic pushed us to discover a lot of new points on the continuum between convenience and personal. What we know best are points that we've experienced, and we were suddenly forced to experience a *lot* of new points. They won't all replace what once was, but we now know those points exist. You can't put them all back in the box and pretend they don't exist. They're out there. Some can get ignored, some can't. It becomes a dance between business and consumer to determine what form the future takes.

The high-touch classroom-based MBA teacher can now do classes online. So, won't the qualified student who doesn't want to commute to the classroom want online access forever? Maybe… but, the learning experience in the classroom is still different. As a school, can you blend the two successfully? How about a hybrid model? Indeed, we are seeing more and more schools offer just that.

One of the big winners during lockdown was Peloton, the 10-year-old, at-home training equipment company that features subscription-based online instructors and workouts. When gyms were closed, many people tried this approach. Purchases skyrocketed, as did the company's stock price. But what did users discover? Some found out that they need (or prefer) a real, live, in-person human instructor to motivate them. Others went back to work and stopped using the subscription altogether. Indeed, for reasons other than pop-culture references, Peloton revenues are decreasing, and its stock price continues to fall. Once a shining example of a substitute solution, Peloton is going back in the box. We'll discuss Peloton further in Chapter 6.

On the other hand, another lockdown beneficiary was the online used-car company Carvana. Anyone else happy to have an option *other* than a used car dealer? Like Peloton, Carvana users were happy to find a decent substitute for an in-person transaction. Unlike Peloton, however, Carvana users seemed *happy* to avoid a human used-car dealer for their needs. Here, there is limited bounce back. Carvana has taken off in popularity, and the observation is permeating the entire retail car industry. Many car manufacturers have already copied Carvana's strategy; shop online, home-delivered new cars are now common. It turns out, not all individuals who buy a car (used or new) want to interact with a human. This limits the level of return we anticipate from this substitute. If consumers like the substitute *better*, it probably won't go back in the box.

However, a computer can't diagnose and repair your car over the internet (yet). So, will the dealer become a full-time repair shop? Substitutes and consumer preferences might give us a glimpse into the future of these industries.

Like the lost human experiences we missed from our bartenders and grooming professionals, some of what we learned from the Covid Pandora's Box was the importance of shared experiences. Watching sporting events with no one in the stands was not the same (piped-in crowd noise was just creepy), and based on 2020/2021 TV ratings for professional football, not as popular. The vicarious aspect of a cheering crowd adds to the enjoyment of watching sports on TV. Indeed, we are seeing ticket sales increase as restrictions loosen.

Of course, not all human experiences changed the same way, nor were they the same for all people. A visit to the doctor became much more detached. Waiting rooms are problematic, so many people have had to resort to seeing a virtual doctor or to be examined in a doctor's parking lot. Allowing for the fact that this might not provide the same quality of medical service as before Covid and similar things were happening before Covid (certainly the virtual office visit), some people might prefer the new, detached approach. In-out-done. Waiting room time is largely useless anyway, and those who are busy and in relatively good health might like the virtual version of a doctor's visit.

Other people might go to the doctor more often and prefer the personal observation and interaction with their medical professionals. Some types of doctor's visits can't be done virtually, especially those with screening and diagnostic testing. So, the ability to put tel-a-doc back in the box varies from person to person. This differential response is similar to our students who want the quality teaching of a high-touch classroom, but don't want the commute. In these cases, Covid gave everyone a chance to figure out what really mattered to them. Priorities changed and preferences are now being commutated.

People, People, People

Pandora's Box might have had its biggest long run impact on the labor market. A large fraction of the labor force learned how to work remotely, and an equally large number of employers learned how important it was to have employees on-site. If the so-called Great Resignation is any indication, the availability of information has had a big impact on employee choices. "Substitutes" for an in-person, on-site job are greater than we thought.

This is not to say that the benefits are one-sided. Indeed, the time an employee saves sprucing up to go to work and commuting to the workplace is now time one could use for many other things (including working more!). Moreover, the wake-up calls about work–life balance, self-management, mental health prioritization, and whether or not they actually like their job made many people quit to search for a situation with a better balance. We'll address this in Chapter 4, but the bottom line is this: once the awareness of a substitute is out there, it's very hard to put it back in the box.

Mini Case: Baskin Robbins

Baskin Robbins built a successful brand on many things that were experiential: free samples, frozen, high-quality ice cream, and at least 31 flavors (they are famous for their 31 flavors). What does a company like this do when, during Covid, samples were (basically) outlawed? How do you rely on delivery of frozen ice cream — just a scoop? — in an Arizona summer? How could Baskin Robbins possibly adapt quickly and survive? Surprisingly, Baskin Robbins came through lockdown well and is now booming. Let's see why.

Baskin Robbins never had a large in-store operation at most of its locations, a couple of tables inside and out. So, transitioning to online ordering and in-store pickup was relatively easy. In addition, Baskin

Robbins teamed up with DoorDash, UberEATS, and Postmates to coordinate home delivery. Getting your ice cream order delivered while it was still frozen was something Baskin Robbins had been working on for a couple of years before Covid, so they were, more or less, road ready when they had to be. Fundamentally, insulated packaging that keeps things cold or frozen is about the same technology as packaging to keep things like pizza hot.

So, the only real loss was in-store sampling. How would that affect the usual offerings of an ice cream store like Baskin Robbins? If they did want to have some new choices among the 31 flavors, how could they change their approach to the new offerings? Ice cream stores do have a bit of an inventory problem. Investigate the "shelf life" of ice cream in an ice cream parlor once the product is opened. Consider the menu at an ice cream parlor. Is there anything on the menu that isn't going to make it in a home delivered, take-home model?

While this isn't something the company is suggesting, are there any cost advantages to keeping the in-store ordering closed forever?

In late 2020, Baskin Robbins was acquired by Inspire Brands. Investigate this new owner and suggest some synergies, perhaps operational, with the various restaurant chains that Inspire owns.

Discussion Questions

2.1 We are here to reconsider our intuition about the business world in the face of Covid. Thinking about the concept of utility maximization, what do you think people learned about the jollies they used to get from going to a café or a pub? Was it all about the coffee or the beer?

2.2 Aside from losing the office for a while, companies also lost things like business trips, retreats, and conferences. Like everything pre-Covid, the importance of those things was taken for granted. How should companies analyze what they've learned because these things weren't possible for a time? What data are needed to accurately assess these things? (Hint: Think Cost-Benefit, SR-LR, the importance of networking, and more....)

2.3 Utility maximization is a balancing act; it isn't as simple as consuming the goods that give you the highest jollies. Why did the "forced test drive" that people experienced (including just "doing without") on dozens of goods that they use every day *negatively* impact some of the well-known brand name products (notably shampoos, razors, and deodorants)? Did any company use the forced test drive to their advantage?

2.4 One thing that a lot of people have learned is the importance of predictability and reliability as a value proposition. But value propositions aren't always straightforward. One of the prime examples of this has, ironically, been the rise of online education. Discuss the value proposition of school and how the move to online education has muddled it.

2.5 Carvana may not end up being the new "model" for buying a car, but it will probably change the old model. Carvana exclusively sells used cars. Many new car dealers are copying Carvana's online shopping, home-delivered approach. So, what (and who) in the traditional car-buying experience is likely to change? (Hint: Think about all aspects of the experience.)

2.6 The virtual doctor's visit is now a "thing." Like many other changes, this was something that already existed and was greatly accelerated by Covid. Discuss the limits of this particular innovation. Consider, for example, the problems with virtual dentistry.

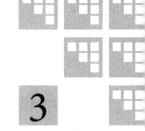

3

Competitive Advantage, Meet Covid

"And on the pedestal these words appear:
'My name is Ozymandias, king of kings;
Look on my works, ye Mighty, and despair!'
Nothing beside remains. Round the decay
Of that colossal wreck, boundless and bare
The lone and level sands stretch far away."

— *Ozymandias, Percy Shelley*

According to many models in economics, "profits" should not be possible in the long run because firms can enter and compete your profits away. Specifically, and depending on the economic model, the combination of more firms and those firms copying everything you do wipes out your profits. But we've seen that long-run profits **do** exist in the real world for some firms even in industries that have many competitors.

The business discipline known as Strategy works to define the elements that make this possible. Strategy amends (one might say, corrects) those economic models by saying there are things that a firm can do to make profits that cannot be copied by competitors. This area of strategy is known as competitive advantage; the real-world sources of sustainable, firm-level profits for what we usually think of as highly successful firms in competitive industries.

Both Strategy and Economics separate competitive advantages into two buckets: consumer-side factors (benefit drivers) and producer-side factors (cost drivers). Let's take a look at both sides.

Benefit Drivers

Benefit drivers are anything that separates your product or service from your competitors, and this can take many forms: the "snob appeal" of high-cost brands; unique designs, flavors, smells, or other sensory features; customer service and convenience, including delivery or free return options; interconnectivity features, like the ability to play TV shows or movies on multiple devices; consistency in quality across multiple regions; and so on. Ask yourself: why do I buy what I buy? If the answer is anything *other* than price alone, you've been motivated by a benefit driver.

One easy example is Apple and its position in the smartphone market. There are about a dozen smartphone manufacturers in the world today, of which Apple is not the biggest. They are not a monopoly, and there is a lot of competition. But, Apple is the most profitable smartphone producer, and they continue to be profitable year after year. How is this possible? Shouldn't competitors be able to compete Apple's profits away?

Well, Apple has quite a few benefit drivers that allow it to price and sell phones at a highly profitable spot on the smartphone demand curve. Apple can charge more than its competitors. Features like integration across multiple platforms, a sleek and durable design, and a high-performing and easy-to-use operating interface make the iPhone a popular choice across demographics and geographic regions. Add to the mix strong brand loyalty, *consistent* pricing, and the allegiance of partner networks across the globe, and you have virtually guaranteed repeat iPhone buyers. Despite the number and proliferation of competitors in major markets, the Apple iPhone remains the most profitable contender in the smartphone industry.

Whenever you see long-term profitable companies in a market that has many competitors, you're seeing the result of at least a few benefit drivers. The market research industry makes billions of dollars determining which benefits are the most appealing to consumers year-to-year, season-to-season, product-to-product. Until Covid, the reliability of the data that underscored these predictions was never really questioned. The appeal and success of benefit drivers changed with the times within predictable parameters.

Predictable, that is, until Covid.

When we look at benefit drivers, there are two key threats to keeping profits in the long run (1) imitation; and (2) changing consumer tastes. To combat imitation, firms typically develop proprietary design features, secret ingredients, well-established brand names with well-maintained reputations, or other factors that the competition really cannot copy, or at least can't copy well. By limiting imitation, these tactics work well as long as consumer preferences don't change.

But consumers change their preferences all the time. Sometimes, they directly change what they like or dislike about a product based on information or trends. Coca Cola's secret formula is a well-known benefit driver (we just won't talk about New Coke and other self-inflicted wounds), but Coke's profits are threatened more and more each year by the movement away from unhealthy, sugary beverages. If a consumer doesn't want sugar and your proprietary formula is mostly sugar, no amount of marketing is going to help drive them to your product reliably in the long run.

Other times, changes in technology drive consumers in a different direction. Blockbuster's once booming success in video rentals was completely upended by the technological innovations that allowed Netflix to stream movies. Streaming is just easier. When consumer preferences changed away from hard copy DVDs, Netflix adapted, and Blockbuster didn't. The technology drove consumers in a different direction.

Trends and technologies have the ability to bend consumer perception and preference over time. Usually, we can see things shifting slowly, but sometimes these changes happen quickly in response to a drastic shock.

Enter Covid.

Let's take a look at the earliest phase of the pandemic when lockdowns began occurring across the world. Lockdowns shifted priorities for consumers in multiple industries. Seemingly overnight, consumers prioritized three things: an increase in personal safety, isolation from large groups, and access to essential goods. Socialization took a back seat to self-preservation. We all saw the results: uncertainty and fear drove consumption decisions, essentials flew off shelves, and drive-through traffic surged. All of a sudden, consumer priorities that were relatively stable and predictable across industries were thrown into question.

Many firms were able to learn things about how durable their benefit drivers are during a shock like the pandemic. They learned quickly whether their existing systems and offerings could adapt to these new consumer priorities. This depended on whether a firm could support itself while this learning curve happened. 2020 and 2021 were make-or-break years for many businesses. We can all recall one or two of our favorite restaurants or boutiques that didn't survive. Competitive advantage notwithstanding, surviving a shock like Covid depends on one thing: cash. A firm must have enough cash reserves to support itself for however long it takes to figure things out and get solutions in place. This could be a week or a year, but bills are due, and the lights have to stay on while development happens.

In essence, the lockdown challenged firms to continue normal business operations while simultaneously "starting over." Very few firms had parked enough cash to survive a year with significantly reduced revenues, and their ability to survive depended on their capacity to cut costs and borrow. Borrowing, of course, depends on the lenders' belief that the firm can recover in reasonably good time. So, now, the effects of the lockdown shock were compounded: both consumer preference and capital partner requirements changed overnight with no indication of an anticipated timeline.

In the US, the federal government helped many businesses by offering loans which became gifts under certain circumstances. This policy did two things. First, it allowed firms to put off decisions until a later time, presumably when things would be clearer and better business decisions could be made. Access to financial resources that do not have to be repaid allowed firms to temporarily ignore — or at least not immediately address — the problems that the pandemic created for them. Second, this delay allowed firms of all sizes to continue to support their employees and vendors in the short run. Understanding that businesses comprise people, these policies kept many firms afloat until the Covid picture could become clearer over subsequent months.

With a temporary solution to cash flow problems, businesses could turn their attention to whether or how to adapt to changed consumer preferences. Covid provided an excellent test of benefit drivers across many industries. Let's talk pizza.

Pizza had long ago become a home-delivered food and the industry knew how to package it in such a way as to maintain most of its desirable features (taste, texture, quality). It was a very small tweak to get drivers to wear masks and make delivery contactless (honestly, the creation of the new word "contactless" was probably harder). The home-delivered pizza industry was in excellent shape to survive the Covid lockdown; it already had the benefit drivers people would desire, so it adapted quickly to the rapid shift in consumer preferences. But, these benefits are also easy to imitate. Given a little time, other restaurants could learn to deliver food straight to your home with about the same quality as the sit-down version. Pizza makers: quick to adapt, easy to copy.

That said, not every restaurant can serve food to your door in a cardboard box. Consider the other end of the restaurant spectrum: high-end, fine-dining establishments. Any restaurant whose benefit drivers are person-to-person, high-touch, and involve the immediate (right out of the kitchen) sense of taste and smell fall under this category. In the lockdown phase, these restaurants suddenly had a problem. Dining is about more than just food and sustenance. It's about ambiance, usually indoors, with lots of personalized expertise, socialization, and interactive service. Let's not forget presentation and plating, which don't translate well to a takeout container.

Sadly, many high-end restaurants simply closed. Virtually every benefit driver that high-end restaurants profited from was disrupted by lockdowns. Not knowing when, where, and how lockdowns would all end, these businesses could not sustain their own workforce, rents, and other costs — even with temporary grants. The shift in consumer preferences went beyond what the restaurants' cash flows could support.

What we know now is that benefit drivers that centered around things that were determined to be risky, like indoor socialization, shared tastes and smells, and highly interactive environments, were the first to be challenged during the pandemic. They remain so because regulations and changing consumer preferences continue to limit predictions for the future. Benefit drivers of taste, smell, and touch have become a liability in many sectors.

Interestingly, having benefit drivers focused on sight and sound created some winners during Covid (we'll discuss this again in Chapter 7). Apple's seamless, free Facetime service only added to the iPhone's appeal and because it only works with other iPhones, Apple sold a lot of smartphones to the geriatric flip-phone crowd. Netflix, Disney+, and other easy-to-use streaming services (with good content) saw their subscriber numbers skyrocket. Convenience, self-preservation, and quality won in the early stages. They "won" when consumer tastes changed. Because of high startup costs, these benefits are also extremely hard to imitate.

What about Zoom? Well, Zoom had a bit of a boom, but showed a big problem early: it's easy to copy and was already copied before the pandemic. By Fall 2020, Microsoft Teams, WebEx, and other online meeting software caught up to the service and offer full integration with existing computer systems. Like pizza delivery, Zoom.com: quick to adapt, easy to copy.

What about other industries, like fashion? Glam brands like Gucci, Rolex, Coach, Ferragamo, and many, many others spent years developing their brand's association with being rich, successful, stylish, and glamorous. In the most derogatory way, marketers refer to this as "snob appeal." You buy the latest scarf or clutch purse on your own, and you can buy them online. So, glam brands shouldn't have had a problem during lockdown, right?

Well, the problem with these brands lies in their benefit drivers: the point of purchasing these items is to show them off to other people. You don't get much pleasure having a pair of Jimmy Choo's on your feet in a Zoom meeting. You look a bit silly holding your arm up all the time in front of your webcam to show off your Rolex watch. And that $280,000 Lamborghini isn't nearly as impressive in your driveway as it was in the company parking lot. The short-term hit that all of these brands took during lockdown was universal. High-cost, experiential brands took a hit across the board, as demand fell, and inventory costs skyrocketed.

Interestingly, though, these losses were short-term. This sector, broadly known as consumer discretionary spending, can be tracked reasonably well in the US by looking at an Exchange Traded Fund (similar to a mutual fund) with the symbol XLY. This fund saw a decrease in value of about 30% in February 2020, but it had recovered all of that by the end of June 2020 — long before we had a vaccine and a couple of months sooner than the rest of the stock market. Why? Arguably there was a belief that Covid would not do any permanent damage to the basic tenets of snob appeal. Unlike food, luxury consumer goods like shoes, purses, cars, and jewelry are storable and durable. While the companies that produce these goods had to take a year off from their usual product cycle (the 2020 Spring Line was not a thing), they were able to save costs and largely weather the storm.

Cost Drivers

Cost drivers are producer-side factors that allow firms to create and maintain long-run profits. Many of these drivers are based on an optimized supply chain. A firm that finds the best way to produce the various inputs it needs usually wins. Calling it a "cost" driver is a bit of a misnomer, as we know producers have to focus on both low-cost and high-quality inputs. In the decades prior to the pandemic, businesses across every industry focused on streamlining and enhancing supply chains; indeed, it has been a business buzz word since the 1990s. However, the supply chain reverberations of Covid have persisted for longer than many of the consumer-side effects. Indeed, as of this writing, supply chain problems are still rampant. Even having optimized supply chains better than ever before, firms the world over are still faced with Covid-related shutdowns. Why?

The natural experiment that we're living is a largely unpleasant one from the producer's perspective. Just as businesses had to contend with unpredictable, rapidly changing consumer preferences, supply chain vendors had to adapt quickly to changing resource needs. In stable markets with predictable demand, most efficient supply chains were focused on their best vendors and thus had very little ability to relocate, redeploy, or rearrange in the short run.

The logistics ballet that was the international shipping system pre-Covid looks now like a game of dodgeball, as every port is backed up and out of sync and half of the transportation conveyances are too empty while the other half are too full.

This particular part of the problem will take years to understand. Arguably, every firm has been impacted by Covid's effect on the supply chain. Simply put, the optimization algorithms were based on a supply and demand system that was relatively balanced. Add a significant shock that disrupts that balance considerably, and the optimization programs will all have to try again with new information.

Just as consumers re-evaluated risk and reward in their decisions, so producers are re-evaluating cost and quality in their supply chain arrangements. Could this shock push input providers closer to end markets so that the supply chain will be more reliable? Could local providers become a more attractive option? These options existed before Covid but were not selected. The system is now being re-evaluated from the top down.

There are other cost drivers that are not related to the supply chain. One that we'll discuss at length in Chapter 4 is corporate culture. Why is it a *cost* driver? Well, it turns out, being an employer that people like working for actually saves the company money. People are less inclined to leave a job that they like, even when they are offered higher pay.

Concept Review: Make vs. Buy

Vertical integration is the question of whether the firm should make or buy its inputs. For any given company, there's an optimization that happens here. For both goods and services, some inputs should be "made" internally, and others should be outsourced. This is the dominant decision businesses have to make, and one that was highlighted from the beginning of the pandemic.

Both Strategy and Economics contribute to the discussion of this concept. While we like to think the make vs. buy decision is based on profit maximization (or more specifically, cost minimization), we know the choice is never clear cut.

Let's review a short list of make vs. buy determinants:

1. *Bureaucracy Cost*: Basically, the costs and problems that arise when vertical integration leads to a cumbersome organizational bureaucracy with no real cost savings. Sometimes called "administrative" costs, it's the time associated with additional red tape, reviews, and oversight that eats away at any efficiencies gained through integration.
2. *Agency Cost*: Springing from the principal–agent problem, these are the costs and problems that arise when a firm tries to produce inputs about which it has no real knowledge or capability. If the firm doesn't know how to evaluate what it's paying for, it will inevitably lose money to inefficiencies and inadequacy.
3. *Coordination Cost*: For some goods, timing is critical in the production process. Vertical integration can usually help in this case, but the savings have to outweigh direct production costs.

4. *Privacy*: If an important part of the firm's value proposition is what we might think of as a "secret formula" that nobody else should know, vertical integration might be necessary.

5. *Transaction Cost*: This is a very big space in economics that, roughly speaking, reminds us that any and every transaction, including buying inputs from a vendor, involves explicit or implicit contracting costs, potential litigation costs, and many other subtle costs. Transaction costs are, arguably, most problematic in the make vs. buy decision when the inputs involved have relationship-specific attributes: things that one customer needs that are specific to that customer and require costly changes in the production of the input. In this case, both the customer and the producer face transaction-specific costs and risks that make the deal more difficult.

6. *Corporate Culture*: While not limited to the make vs. buy decision, corporate culture is a critical element to cost minimization when the firm is considering vertically integrating. This is usually associated with services where the "primary" service of a firm is valued more than "support." Corporate culture will be discussed at length in Chapter 4.

Consider a firm that had achieved competitive advantage by optimally determining which input services to make and which ones to buy and assume that what they decided to make internally worked best with a certain amount of human interaction. A restaurant that had its own pastry chef succeeded because that chef could adapt the desserts to the main menu. An in-house marketing firm can learn things by talking to the design people. Cost savings here were rooted in institutional knowledge, workforce synergies, connections between staff. These are major cost drivers and extremely hard to imitate. Even if a competitor "buys away" your best talent, integration with the new team would take a long time to build.

Yet, these cost savings depended on the situation that existed pre-Covid; pre-lockdown; pre-mask. The detachment of the new workplace (not to mention the Great Resignation) disrupted a lot of these pre-Covid synergies and erased a lot of institutional connections. In some cases, firms had to switch from make to buy for some services, finding themselves hiring consultants who are expensive, not as well-connected, and detached from the team just to get the job done.

Here, supply chain disruptions are testing many cost drivers. One could say that logistics is the art and science of minimizing coordination costs, but that minimization, even if it's done with a certain amount of wiggle room, could not prepare for what firms are currently experiencing.

The Great Resignation has been a powerful test of a firm's ability to find new skilled employees, and in many ways it is testing firm strategies for dealing with agency costs. Among the components of agency cost that firms always deal with are monitoring costs. For many firms with long-term employees, the work-at-home mandates were relatively innocuous. Experienced, seasoned employees could be trusted to get work done even when they were outside the office. New, replacement hires are, by definition, untested. Even the factors that a firm looked for in new hires changed. Before Covid, firms could simply look for someone with the right technical skill set for a job. Now, it's time to find people with the right skill set who are good at self-management and need minimal oversight. As any recruiter will tell you, this changes the game considerably.

With significant shifts in both benefit and cost drivers, businesses are facing a new and uncertain future. Competitive advantage has, predictably, favored companies that were doing a lot of things well. In addition, as we'll see in Chapter 7, some companies that had competitive advantages that were well positioned arguably got stronger, during the Covid years. But the pandemic changed the game quickly — too quickly for businesses to adapt sustainably well. The results will be long lasting and discussed for years to come.

Mini Case: Tesla

"For want of a nail, the shoe was lost, for want of a shoe, the horse was lost, and for want of a horse, the battle was lost." This is a version of an old proverb that has never been more relevant. The supply chain disruptions that we've seen as the world emerged from the Covid lockdowns were often the sort that resonate with this expression.

Ford Motor Company, General Motors, and most auto manufacturers had to idle manufacturing plants around the world for lack of computer chips that are critical to the modern automobile's operation. In the modern, optimized supply chain, the key to sourcing your inputs is cost minimization. But saving a few dollars on a computer chip by sourcing it in Taiwan has ultimately cost the auto industry millions of dollars in sales of new cars.

While some of those customers are more or less waiting to buy their new car, others opted for alternatives like used cars. Regardless, deferred sales still represent lost money.

Interestingly, Tesla was able to navigate the chip shortage much better than its auto industry rivals. Let's posit that Tesla is the future of the industry. Aside from its all-electric motor, what other fundamental differences in Tesla allowed it to avoid the auto industry's chip dip? Since Tesla is the "new(ish) kid on the block, how did its ability to navigate the chip shortage help it achieve sales of almost a million cars in 2021? Specifically, investigate the way Teslas are sold. You should see a big difference between buying a Tesla and buying most other cars in the US. So how did the chip shortage and its ramifications at every other car dealer end up helping Tesla with what might be its biggest drawback?

Discussion Questions

3.1 Many companies are reconsidering their supply chain because of the shortages that they experienced during the Covid era. Product outages give customers a reason to try alternatives and learn about how much they really need a particular good. We've focused on when this is bad for the incumbent. Can it ever be good?

3.2 Supply chain issues exist across most market sectors. Does this mean manufacturing jobs that left years ago for China, Canada, and other countries will be returning to the US? (Hint: Look at wage rates.)

3.3 Benefit and Cost Drivers are there for the labor market, too. How have costs and benefits changed for people in the service sector since May 2020? What about tradespeople? What about healthcare workers? Teachers? Architects? IT professionals? What about law enforcement?

Accountants? Veterinarians? Why are the costs and benefits different for these groups? What drives drivers?

3.4 Can you think of a fast-food restaurant chain or some thing similar whose benefit drivers were likely disrupted by the forced test drives that Covid created?

3.5 We've argued that small, high-touch colleges and similar education providers had their benefit drivers seriously impacted by the Covid lockdowns. Does any part of their benefit drivers actually improve with the move online?

4

High Noon: Corporate Culture

"Choose a job you love, and you will never have to work a day in your life."
— *Confucius*

In the dramatic climax of the classic film *High Noon*, the town marshal, having vanquished the bad guys with no help from the cowering citizenry, looks at the gathered townsfolk with disgust, throws his badge into the dirt, and rides away (with Grace Kelly, so we don't exactly feel sorry for him). Throughout this movie we get to see why someone does something dangerous or difficult — and why they stop. It's a combination of talent and inner drive to do the right thing. Something has to inspire and sustain that inner drive. One thing that does that in the business world is what we call Corporate Culture.

Corporate culture is the real reason, other than a paycheck, people work for your company as opposed to other companies. It is why people work for you, and why they perform and produce beyond the level necessary to keep their job (or as economists would say, the value of the marginal product of labor — the level of output necessary to "pay" for their job).

It is an economic fundamental that an employee's wage has to be less than or equal to the value of their productivity in order to justify having that job. But, employers have learned that employees are not simply the embodiment of a calculus derivative; they are people. Emotional, passionate, people who on a good day have to actually like what they're doing for a living. Productivity, especially in the modern workplace where many rote jobs are being done by robots, involves levels of effort. Getting the most out of an employee requires that the employer respect and maybe even inspire workers. This is where corporate culture matters.

Concept Review: Tribal Culture

Culture, in a non-yoghurt sense, is the norms, standards, rules, languages, and other things that organize societies. When we grow up in a country, we usually take these things for granted. We assume they exist for a good reason if we think about them at all. Many of these things are ingrained in us during our childhood: respect your elders, respect authority, religious dogma (see the Ten Commandments), and many other things.

Anthropologists call this "tribalism," and there's a certain amount of tribalism in all societies. Pecking orders, rituals, and contests all have ancient roots, but we can see remnants of these systems in our modern societies. Each of our tribes — and we have many, and they often build on each other — has its own languages and beliefs, and these can change as you move between tribes. You don't usually talk to your mother the same way you talk to your boss. You don't talk to your husband the way you talk to your local barista.

Consider the tribe known as mathematicians. Like other academic disciplines, they have a pecking order (PhD from MIT or Cal Tech, PhD from anywhere else, Master's Degree, Bachelor's Degree, ordinary human). Yes, academics are all that pretentious. Let's just take that as a given. Mathematicians have contests and trophies (Google: Math Awards!), and they most definitely have their own language. If you were to happen upon a conversation between theoretical mathematicians, you would probably believe they were speaking gibberish. To borrow a line from humorist (and mathematician) Tom Lehrer's song *Lobachevsky*, "It was on analytic and algebraic topology of locally Euclidean parameterization of infinitely differentiable Riemannian manifold." We rest our case.

Most people have had the experience of watching something on the National Geographic channel about strange (to us) tribes in various parts of the world that have resisted (or been removed from) the changes we often call "the modern world" and continue to embrace ancient customs around a communal fire. This is just another tribe, but one you might honestly understand better than mathematicians. You might feel similarly "out of place" in a throng of football fans if you don't like sports or going to dinner with a new group of people that you've never met. In truth, all tribes have "goofy" rituals; to not see this is evidence of our own closed-mindedness.

Tribal culture has a purpose: connection. Connection with others in a group creates credibility (although not always well-deserved; consider conspiracy theorists). Having a tribe allows for easier internal communication because you all speak the same language. It creates order out of chaos by providing a structure of norms. On the other hand, tribal culture can be rife with "isms" and phobias. Notorious among them: sexism, racism, ageism, and xenophobia.

There has been a good deal of social discourse and discord in the US over the past two years about cultures, norms, and "isms." This kind of shake-up is normal and healthy in most cases. It reminds us to consider those who feel more like "them" as opposed to "us." We need to remind ourselves that all of the rules and norms we take for granted were our invention and, even if they meant well, they are not perfect and they are not carved in stone. With some reflection and understanding of the impact that our norms and rules have, our tribal cultures can and should evolve.

Corporate culture represents the "tribe" within a corporation. It's a part of the tribes of your profession and your industry, which have norms, too. Every group has its own standards, rules, languages, and other things. For outsiders, a particularly frustrating part of corporate lingo is acronyms and catchphrases. Think about how quickly you forget that no one outside of your workplace knows what a "CV from a PhD in Comp Lit" is. RFPs mean something very different from industry to industry. Certifications and registrations are unique to a particular group of professionals. At least once a year, a PhD will have to say, "no, I'm not that type of doctor." Corporate lingo matters.

Until they are challenged by external norms (like the aforementioned social push to eliminate sexism or racism), internal corporate norms are assumed to be an important part of a firm's success. Paying your dues, hierarchy, hiring standards — all of the things that are part of corporate culture — are in place for a reason. Hiring standards in particular can be insidious. "Not our kind of person," and other clubbish standards end to make the firm difficult for new people. Once you're immersed in a job, a company, and its culture, you know what you know, and you don't know what you don't know. You will learn and connect and be productive. But none of that happens if you don't get the job.

A major, economy-wide shift in production processes can re-inform employers and employees alike. Women in the manufacturing workplace were uncommon in the US before World War II, but when the War forced men to leave jobs to join the armed forces, manufacturers had to turn to a new workforce. Turns out, women filled the need quickly and defense contractors were able to produce plenty of tanks and planes for the war effort.

When the war was over, many women left the workforce, but the knowledge they had about this experience and their story lived on. This paved the way for a larger, more permanent role for women in the workplace a few decades later. Two things had to happen before women became permanent members of the workforce. Women had to want the jobs — the World War II experience helped that immeasurably — and corporate culture had to change. Once the war was over and the defense imperative was gone, these took longer.

When we talk about culture in the workplace, we know we're talking about amorphous concepts that are difficult to measure. Under normal circumstances, an employer's best test of its corporate culture is employee turnover. Every firm and industry had metrics on how often they have to hire and retrain for positions. In a perfect world, a company tries to find a balance between employee turnover and the cost of replacement.

A restaurant probably doesn't worry quite as much about losing their dishwasher as it does losing its head chef. Hospitals probably worried more about losing doctors and nurses than receptionists. A law firm worries more about losing partners than losing clerks. This isn't a commentary on the value of the individual, but on the industry's *perception* of the value of the individual given the turnover of the day and the current labor market. The values above were all pre-Covid. What if all the dishwashers, nurses, and law clerks quit at the same time?

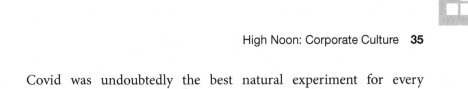

Covid was undoubtedly the best natural experiment for every employer's corporate culture that we've seen in a long time. Even the best employers forget how they got there. Hierarchies, rules, standards, promotions, and so on. Many aspects of corporate culture depend on a certain *lack* of knowledge on the part of employees. Low-level employees who assumed their job was the best they could achieve. Covid's Pandora's Box from employee's perspective highlighted many things that firms did not want employees to know.

In late 2021, we realized nobody wanted to go back to work at restaurants. Why? Many jobs at restaurants pay well if you include tips. Many of these jobs involve on-the-job training rather than formal schooling, so the entry point is within reach of almost everyone. People still want to go out to eat (or at least pick up food), so demand is there. Why not go back?

Well, ask people who worked at a restaurant about their experience. Ask a person who did a stint as part of the wait-staff. Or just think about that often-thankless job from the perspective of the customer. The wait staff's tip ultimately depends on the performance of most of the rest of the restaurant's employees. The best waitperson in the world will be under-tipped if the people in the kitchen don't cook the steak correctly. (And let's face it, there's no well-accepted definition of medium rare). Add to this a tense service environment, mask mandates, and the overarching threat of catching a communicable disease, and we have a problem finding people to fill the wait staff role.

Underappreciated health care workers would tell a similar story. Hospital hierarchies are very, very top-down: Doctors, Physician Assistants, Nurse Practitioners, Registered Nurses, other nurses, other health care workers. It is what it is, until everyone is suddenly overworked and the pecking order stress falls on the lowest couple of tiers. Even if they were suddenly being paid more, they still got very little respect. Many of them quit and are still quitting. It's a theme that has echoed across many sectors in the US economy and abroad.

In the News

At a macro level, these changes in the labor market have been called The Great Resignation and The Big Quit. Figure 4.1 shows the dramatic

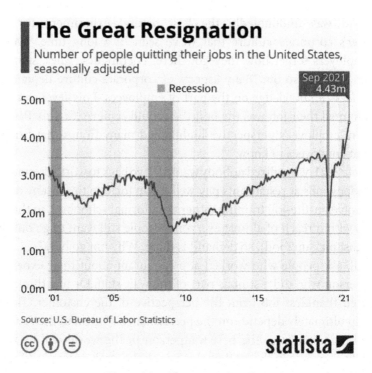

Figure 4.1: The great resignation

increase in the number of people who quit their jobs in 2021, and by all accounts, that has continued into early 2022. There are a lot of reasons and explanations for this, not all having to do with Covid. In addition, some industries such as hospitality and health care appear to be more affected than others by trend. As more data are accumulated and more research can be done on this anomaly, it will be interesting to see how much of The Great Resignation is due to some aspect of corporate culture.

Corporate culture, that tribal world of the firm that keeps people coming back, is extremely general. Loosely, it's why people keep working well and keep working for you. Changes that affect culture can happen all at once (like Covid), or over time. They can affect just one thing, like wages, or everything at once (again, like Covid). Nobody wants to hear the term "circle back" anymore. Nobody wants to keep blaming the supply chain. A lot of people want to keep working well, and keep working for you, but they don't want to come back to the office anymore. That's where we go next.

Mini Case: McDonald's

McDonald's was a pioneer in the fast-food industry. While it does have "company owned" stores, most McDonald's are franchised, individually owned businesses. Among its many claims to fame is McDonald's reputation as a place where people could get their first job.

If you include all of the franchisees in the US, McDonald's employs about 2 million people, making it one of the country's top five private employers. But there's another side of this story. McDonald's has always had high labor turnover. So, the Great Resignation wasn't quite as big a shock to McDonald's. Indeed, they have some advantages. They had a lot of experience on-boarding new employees and many of their jobs required very little skill. Even so, McDonald's had to increase wages and other benefits in many places in order to maintain their labor force.

As a fast-food, take-out oriented company with drive-up service at most of its restaurants, McDonald's had advantages during the Covid years. But arguably, an employee-friendly corporate culture is not one of them. Investigate and compare the reputation of McDonald's to some of its (admittedly newer and smaller) competitors in the US like In-n-Out and Chick-fil-A.

Chick-fil-A, is a franchise restaurant. In-n-Out is not. Why might this matter? In particular, why is it more difficult in general to change the corporate culture of a franchise operation?

McDonald's solution to the Great Resignation was to increase pay and benefits; to increase its costs. If they could have found a way to adjust their corporate culture, this might not have been necessary. But the company was moving in a different direction for a couple of years before Covid. What technological changes was McDonald's making to mitigate higher labor costs even before Covid hit? Given that, why was their much-hyped increase in pay in 2021 something McDonald's wasn't that concerned about?

Discussion Questions

4.1 The problem with corporate culture is you don't get opportunities to test how good it is without serious consequences. Inertia, needing the paycheck (sometimes called golden handcuffs), and simply wanting to stay in a comfort zone keep many people from leaving jobs — even if they hate them. Outside of the seismic shock of Covid, how can organizational leaders assess corporate culture on a regular basis?

4.2 It's not all about ping-pong tables in the break room and flexible PTO. What are the elements of corporate culture you value? Where did these things come from and how did they change over the past few years?

4.3 Information is key, especially for firms. Put yourself in an employer's shoes. You want to do right by your employees, but they're leaving in droves. What do you need to *know* to stop the losses?

4.4 Turnover is inevitable; those entering the workforce 60 years ago were expected to stay with the same firm forever. Twenty years ago, you were expected to change jobs 3–4 times. Those professionals entering now are expected to have at least three *careers* over their lifetime. Change happens. What makes people crave change in the professional environment, and how has Covid affected these factors?

4.5 Law firms, architecture firms, engineering firms, and other similar skill-based organizations usually have employees (even departments) that do things like marketing, finance, and human resources. Suppose you are the founder and a managing partner at a firm like that and you noticed that half of your marketing department quit during the Great Resignation. What would you do per your corporate culture?

5

Office Lost

"The most important thing in communication is to hear what isn't being said."

— *Peter Drucker*

Organizational Behavior (OB) is a curiously named business discipline. We often think of behaviors as organic, how a person or animal acts under various stimuli. Organizations are esoteric things, not individual people, per se. But OB tries to explain how an organization composed of people will operate. The military has had an excellent sense of the tenets of organizational behavior for centuries. The importance of rigidity, teamwork, and selflessness define organizations like the US Marine Corps. Other organizations thrive by motivating creativity, independence, and individuality.

OB can focus on a particular industry, regulatory environment (think different national laws), and organizational structure. It will even look at the differences between organizations within the same ecosystem. The goal of this area of study is to look at the conditions under which certain behaviors happen, and whether these behaviors elicit any type of predictable successes or failures. In this way, OB has become a mainstay of management programs around the world.

OB post-Covid, however, is very much a work in progress. It bears repeating that the lessons we are learning from Covid are not all complete. It will take decades to study and understand what worked — literally — and what didn't in the "great rearrangement" that Covid caused in every business. But we can talk about a few OB-related things that are already clear.

OB scholars like to refer to the "organic" processes that underlie this area of study. Since they're really looking at how natural processes affect made-up organizations, this is just a fancy way of saying "let's see what happens." In this area, we are interested in things like synergy, reporting structures, remote work capabilities, training programs, promotion protocols, the value of education, tribalism, and communication. We talked about some of these in Chapter 4, but we saved the best topic for this chapter: communication. Without it, all operations within an organization would cease immediately.

Within the human body, communication is what keeps us alive. Brain cells tell heart cells to beat, lung cells to breath, and stomach cells to digest. As they showed during the French Revolution, quickly removing the communication link between the brain and these other organs pretty much ends the life of that particular human.

When we talk about communication in the broadest sense, we have to acknowledge that it has undergone significant upheaval anyway, and it continues to change at an increasing rate. Some forms of communication within an organization move naturally with innovation. Telephones, beepers, the internet, email, smartphones, texting, and a long list of other communication changes have been part of everyone's life. Those of you reading this book learned how to communicate from different starting points; some of you probably grew up with an iPhone in hand, while others (like one writer of this book) saw their first computer in the third grade. Still others (like another writer of this book) have no idea what an emoji is. Communication changes all the time. What we want to look at here is how the traditionally accepted forms of communication changed drastically in the face of the Covid pandemic.

Two things happened to communication as the pandemic shut down offices. First, companies lost the environment in which communication traditionally happened. Second, it increased dependency on other forms of communication (e.g., media/mediums) that forced the entire firm ecosystem (managers & employees) to learn a new "language" quickly. Let's take a look at each of these issues.

Non-Verbal Communication

An underappreciated mode of human interaction that was changed (maybe even completely lost) when people began working at home is non-verbal communication. Virtual meetings are great. We didn't really wear pants for a year. On the other hand, it is very hard (impossible?) to interpret body language over Zoom. At best, you get facial expressions, and even then, only if everyone's camera is turned on. No more sensing an employee tense up when you mention that difficult client. No more running and hiding when you see the boss coming or nodding to your work bestie when that other annoying coworker walks by. What's more, you now can see your own face during virtual meetings! Communicative facial expression tends to be spontaneous and uncorrected. Seeing yourself on the computer screen allows you to undo many responses. The non-verbal cues that underpin the tribal culture and communication infrastructure of the office were suddenly gone.

We don't think about how important non-verbal communication is most of the time. Smiles, frowns, eye contact, and other facial reactions convey a lot of information. Body language like gesturing, how one walks, slumped shoulders, or sprinting through the office tells coworkers a lot about your mood and your attitude. Does it always have to do with work? No, but it's still important. Are your employees burnt out? Needing help rarely starts with asking for help. Are they excited to be working for you? Being disenchanted never starts when someone quits. The first forms of communication are often non-verbal.

In taking away the office culture, however briefly, Covid shutdowns removed the non-verbal cues that underpin the tribal culture and communication infrastructure.

Like non-verbal communications, casual conversation also includes important information. Chats among co-workers in the break room or at lunch (or euphemistically at the water cooler, which was always creepily unhygienic, and we're surprised they lasted that long anyway) might be the first hint of a problem or the first place someone mentions a potentially interesting new idea. Strategists like to talk about synergy, where an idea has greater potential than the sum of its parts. Well, synergy usually starts with a casual conversation.

Realistically, all of these lost conversations have positives and negatives. Some casual communication can waste time. Some conversations at work aren't about work. Rumors, gossip, flirting, joking, the NCAA Basketball Tournament betting pool, and of course, politics are all part of office conversation. But before we say things are "better" without the timewasters, ask yourself: what really connects people to their organization? What makes a team a team? What makes a tribe a tribe?

We generally believe that it's easier to focus on work if no one can drop by our office to chat. But is that really better? Clearly that depends on the task and the situation one has at home. All the parents out there: has working from home always been an ideal, calm environment for you to concentrate? For everyone: how much have you experienced loneliness and isolation?

For employers, none of this is easy to identify — because you can't see it. OB, as a discipline, is just getting started on finding reliable answers. Let's be honest, we can't wait for academia to figure it out. After all, it's a lot easier for employees to search for a new job when they're doing it unnoticed at home all day.

Matching Medium to Message

We have mentioned that Covid changed many things, and that it simply accelerated changes that were already underway prior to the pandemic. The loss of the office environment really falls into the latter category. Communication methods and media have been changing as they always have, as new technologies, apps, and platforms become available to the masses. Covid really pushed us to examine what works better under a particular circumstance: how to perform as part of a team while remaining in isolation.

It used to be that some communications — important and not — were verbal in the office and in person. Many of those are now made over email, virtual meetings, or via texts. We were already using these digital communications more each year, but they are now the *only* form of communication for some people who work together. That means every email and every text is now getting lost in the flood. What we have here, literally, is a failure to communicate.

Well, maybe.

Two things are important in effective communication: what information are you trying to convey (message) and how are you going to get it to your target (medium). These two have to match. You text your husband to ask about dinner, but you (usually) don't text the President of your company a $$$ emoji to ask for a raise. You email your daughter's teacher the signed permission slip for the upcoming field trip, but signing your tax return takes a secure, password-protected connection verified with your social security number, bank routing number, prior years unique pin, the street you grew up on, and the name of your first dog. Message and medium matter.

This digital information flood is, in most ways, a poor substitute for the myriad non-verbal forms of communication that it replaced. There are dozens of emoticons that can be attached to an email or a text but they don't carry the same weight as the in-person communication that they substitute for. Because the medium has changed from in-person to virtual, the messages run the risk of being lost. We have all, in essence, had to convert or completely relearn our traditionally accepted modes of communication in the workplace. This has challenged leaders — both formal and informal — of all organizations to help guide the tribe back to functionality.

Concept Review: Modes of Leadership

Teaching leadership is trickier than teaching most other business skills. While arguably all business skills should all be taught with a humanist inclination (businesses are people, after all), finance, accounting, and operations are fundamentally math-based. Leadership, not so much. There's also a certain skepticism on the part of students and others. Some say leadership can't be taught; leaders are born, not made. Nothing could be further from the truth, but this isn't the place to have that debate.

Leadership is less of a personality trait and more of a social influence thing. Put differently, we prefer to talk about *modes of leadership*. To be a leader, people have to follow you. More specifically: people have to follow you *willingly*. Leadership is not the same thing as power. That people do things because you can threaten them is not leadership, that's just official control and power over the individual. Watch Spartacus (or Gladiator) enough times and you begin to see how power tends to lose in the face of a true leader.

There are many modes of leadership. Let's consider a few that are accepted and well understood:

1. *Directive* leadership is what we think of as giving orders. As a form of leadership (not power), this is usually associated with necessary expedience (first responders, surgeons, military leaders, etc.), having knowledge and specific skills (supervisors, coaches, parents), or a combination of both.
2. *Transactional* leadership involves various forms of rewards and punishments. You experience transactional leadership when you do something because you get paid or praised. You also see it when you decide not to do something because you might get yelled at or fired.
3. *Transformational* leadership involves inspiration, growth, a sense of serving a higher-purpose, and other non-pecuniary things that a job might give. Transformational leaders are often ones that we associate with terms like "charisma". There is a well-known personality archetype associated with transformational leadership, and that is usually what people mean when they say leaders are born not made. However, people can be trained to be more charismatic. Plus, charisma does not always mean somebody can be a good leader. For transformational leadership, some sort of charisma is necessary, but not sufficient.
4. *Empowering* leadership involves delegating leadership for some things to the individual. Empowering leaders will teach employees, inspire action, and advocate for them to self-manage. This mode of leadership includes mentoring and training, creating a shared vision, delegating tasks, and minimizing micromanagement of followers.

Like medium and message, modes of leadership have to be matched with the organizational structure of the firm. What's sometimes called a flat hierarchy or shared leadership is used in highly, diversely skilled organizations. In these cases, every different skill is crucial, and all employees are expected to take a leadership role. Here, we expect to see a more transformational or empowered form of leader emerge. Each employee has to "find their voice" and at the same time, the organization has to listen. On the other hand, more dictatorial hierarchies emerge in firms that depend on uniformity and repetitiveness (think manufacturing). Diversity isn't as necessary as consistency, and employees are expected to follow a single set of parameters. So, we expect to see a more directive, transactional approach. Each employee can clock in, work, clock out, and get paid. There is no need to find a voice or approach to get the best job done.

When Covid forced the loss of the office environment, it also pushed firms to change modes of leadership. When employees had to work at home or in a completely new setting, directive and transactional modes became less effective and sometimes even counterproductive. Physically detaching the employee from the organization removed small but important moments that allowed transactional leadership to work. Those little pats on the back or smiles of approval simply weren't there. Heavy-handed directive or paycheck-only transactional leadership rarely work in the modern workplace, and they work even less during an environmental shock.

Very few leaders had the ability to look at their post-Covid workplace and quickly determine how to change modes of leadership to deal with the events that occurred. Although we know it can be taught, leadership is an iterative process: you learn how to be a good leader slowly, with lessons over time. Consider a gregarious waitperson who enjoyed interacting with patrons at a sit-down restaurant. In a well-run eatery, this person is the conduit between the kitchen, the customer, and management. If things go well, they are reasonably well-paid (tips!) and they feel respected by everyone concerned. This person has been empowered to be a leader. Now, how do they feel when they simply run Styrofoam containers of food out to the parking lot? This is a very different job. The environment of empowerment is no longer there. Is there anything management can do to make it better?

Unfortunately, the leadership aspects of the post-Covid world only showed how poorly trained a lot of people were in understanding the importance of applying the right mode of leadership for a particular situation at a particular time. At the extreme, the Great Resignation is about workforce abuse, but it is also about the loss of workforce celebration and empowerment. Yes, the pandemic exposed how some disciplines were treated badly. But, it also exposed how some disciplines could no longer thrive, even as work needed to continue.

As we'll discuss in greater detail in Chapter 8, an office lost also means boundaries are lost. Boundaries include the things that keep the home environment and work environment separate. Once upon a time, if someone working at your office went home sick — visibly, obviously sick — you wouldn't send them home with a stack of papers and more work to do. They're home sick. But what happens when you work from home... sick? If you're "allowed" to work from home, many are still expected to work. That's an interesting problem to sort out. One could argue that, unless you are incapacitated, you could do some work. But who's to say what's reasonable? After all, pre-Covid, people did do some work from home including when they were sick. Some people like not losing a paycheck if they can push through a flu without being a risk to others. Where does productivity come in? We'll talk about this in a few chapters.

Looking at office lost, though, there are so many more issues. First, it's true that you can't go home from work if you're working from home, but you also can't "escape" your home if you don't have an office. It's naïve to think that everyone who worked from home during the Covid lockdown was happier doing so. For some people, the office was an escape that helped reset some daily stresses.

On the other hand, some working people are getting what might be their first first-hand experience in what happens at home. For families that have one working partner and one stay-at-home partner, a lot of "how was your day" conversations have been rendered moot. It's now shared experience. It remains to be seen whether this is good, bad, or just different from a family perspective. If you believe that more information is always better, it could be a good thing.

Interesting Aside

There's a tendency to separate the humanist and quantitative aspects of business. We usually teach about people in classes on leadership and OB and math in classes like finance, accounting, and quantitative methods. Classes like strategy try to integrate these areas, but even then, they are somewhat separated depending on what topic you're covering.

If the business world learned anything from COVID-19, it's that success takes an understanding of both human and quantitative elements. There is an interesting example of this that has come to light recently: Angel Investing.

When an entrepreneur starts a business, they need money to get the business off the ground. There will usually be a formal business plan with lots of numbers; accounting and finance things that show that — if everything goes well — the business will be able to pay back early investors. Because this stage of the start-up is hypothetical and there's lots of uncertainty about the new product's future revenues, early investors are taking a lot of risks. Most start-ups fail, and early investors usually lose their money.

Early investors are also called Angel Investors (think Shark Tank), and they use a variety of approaches in deciding how to invest their money. Of course, they diversify — they invest in many different start-ups. Diversification is a tried-and-true investment strategy. Really successful Angel Investors also use their instincts a lot. Instincts, in this case, take many forms. Does the Angel Investor agree about the future market potential of the new product? What about customers? Does the Angel Investor see the tenacity, leadership ability, and vision in the entrepreneur that is necessary for the new product to succeed? What instinctual reaction do you have to the person asking for money? There's no equation or algorithm for instinct, but it is a very real part of the investor's decision-making process. Angel Investors have said they will look at the numbers and discuss that quantitative aspect of the start-up, but ultimately make their investment when they shake the entrepreneur's hand and look in their eyes. Which, thanks to Covid, they can't really do as much as they used to.

Non-verbal communication is an important part of a lot of business, including things we *thought* were fully quantitative, like finance and accounting. Future research might well show that Angel Investing declined during the Covid era, specifically during the lockdown phase when face-to-face meetings were hard to do. The uncertainties of Covid and its impact on the future economy would have interfered with Angel Investors' instincts about the market, too. The public trading markets, NASDAQ, NYSE, etc., arguably provide more real-time data than any other investment medium in the world. Even then, we see changes in investment patterns based on changes in human instincts.

Mini Case: Google

Many tech companies began reeling in their workforce at the beginning of 2022, offering many employees a hybrid schedule but telling them they should be in the office a couple of days a week. Some companies, like Microsoft and Google, are giving minimum days of the week in the office but leaving workers to choose which days. Others, like Apple, are specifying which days employees have to be in the office.

In all cases, tech firms face a combination of problems and issues when their employees work from home. Lost synergies, security and privacy problems, lack of oversight, and the aforementioned inability to tell when employees are unhappy at work. Turnover is not uncommon in the tech industry. Highly skilled workers are also highly sought after. Difficult work environments are not uncommon and the workforce on average is very young compared to many other industries.

But the Great Resignation hit many of these tech titans hard. Google, the main business platform of holding company Alphabet, was no exception. But Google was one of the Silicon Valley firms that made free meals, employee playgrounds, and work-on-your-own-thing days part of a unique, to the outside observer, employee-friendly corporate culture. What happened?

Research Google's reputation and rankings as an employer from their employee's perspective. While they are usually considered a very good employer, they are a tech-first company where other skills such as business skills (finance, marketing, strategy, etc.) are not viewed as equals by many IT and engineering people.

That's not uncommon, but a shared sense of accomplishment can smooth over many such problems. In addition, having the ability to spend time with colleagues working on projects of your own with the full support of Google is a great perk.

Also, highly technical, specialized jobs tend to be more well-suited to work-from home, with limited in-person collaboration needed. Indeed, your research should have found issues along those lines among the criticisms of Google's culture. So, pull all of this together and tell a story about why Google, one of the techiest of tech companies, wants its people to come back to the office.

Discussion Questions

5.1 To whatever extent the Great Resignation is due to missed, perhaps non-verbal, communications, what could team, department, and organizational leaders do to mitigate that in a future without in-person interaction? What's the biggest downside of your suggestion?

5.2 Even before Covid, companies tried to recreate office dynamics remotely, trying to unite people working in different office locations across the nation or world. By all accounts, this had limited success. Did the pandemic hurt or help this type of communication? When all of your employees are working remotely, how did this help or hinder cross-office integration? (Hint: Languages, time zones, cultures.)

5.3 Given your answer to Question 5.2, how effective is remote connection in light of increased employee turnover?

5.4 If your leadership style had been primarily transactional (raises, bonuses, promotions, etc.) and that was appropriate for your employees and their tasks, do you have to move to more empowerment now? If so, what will have to be true for this to succeed? (Hint: Think about what employees value in each type.)

5.5 Between the lost forms of communications, the need for social distancing, and other changes in the workplace, organizations are all starting over. Suggest new ways for companies to foster collaboration that can survive in a world that might always have to deal with shocks like Covid.

5.6 What jobs can be done at home? When does the company worry about risks to its product from work at home?

6

Lucky or Good?

"Fortune brings in some boats that are not steered."
— *Cymbeline, William Shakespeare*

Finding success has always been unpredictable in the business world. The nature of innovation is that some new things hit the market at just the right time, during a confluence of demand, technology, and supply chain availability. Others — some of them great ideas — wither on the vine waiting for the fates to align. Covid rather famously breathed new life into a few companies that were struggling to find success, but that doesn't mean that these companies were all "great." Looking at success during the pandemic, we have to separate two things: opportunism and fundamentals. Is success durable or fleeting? Are these companies good or just lucky?

Invention is the creation of a new product or service. Innovation is the act of bringing this new product or service to market. These are two very different things. Invention relies on creation, testing, and improvement on what happened before. Innovation relies on identifying a need and how to serve it that will help both the consumer and you, the producer.

When a new product hits the market, a producer makes an educated guess about what people will be willing to pay and how many units can be sold at that price. This is a demand curve, and a producer ties to predict what it looks like. To say a company "failed" means it was wrong about where a new product will end up on the demand curve. It couldn't accurately predict what the new product's actual price should be nor how much it would sell in the short and long runs. From there, the numbers don't add up, and the producer goes under.

If the need is established and the market for the product is clear, a producer can look at the price of close substitutes as a starting point. From there, a company can declare its benefit or cost drivers through marketing and advertising. Maybe it's "ours is as good as the famous name brand but at half the price" (like, Harry's Razors), or "ours has most of the features of the other one but it's prettier and easier to use and has more snob appeal" (Apple's iPhone). Once the demand is determined and the attributes are clear, promotion is the missing piece of the innovation puzzle.

But the ultimate arbiter of a product's success is the consumer. Consumers will map out the *actual* prices and how much they're willing to buy. Consumers determine the *actual* demand curve. This reality has to align with cost of production. Every project has to pass the Net Present Value test in order to survive. The product has to generate enough profits in the long run to pay for the upfront cost of producing it. The new canned soup company has to be able to sell enough cans of soup at a profit over time in order to pay off the loan they took out to build the canned soup factory. The neighborhood coffee shop has to make enough in sales to pay rent, pay its employees, and repay its start-up loan. If the demands for soup or coffee don't support the costs of production, these companies both go bankrupt.

Concept Review: Economies of Scale

One potential long-run savior for these or any business that has a sudden increase in sales is what economists call Economy of Scale. To survive, a business must eventually get to a point where its price is greater than or equal to its average cost. Average cost is a difficult hurdle. It includes variable cost things like raw materials, labor, and utilities and fixed cost things like your factory or shop, your machinery, and other important factors. These factors are sometimes called "fixed capital."

The economics of a business' short- and long-run success usually goes something like this:

- In the short run, you try to sell units at a price that covers the cost of producing the last unit you sell. For our economics aficionados, this is marginal revenue. You're aware of the fact that early on, you're going to lose money because of the upfront cost of your fixed factors — but you try not to lose more money than that amount. Economists say you want price to cover marginal cost in the short run.

- In the long run, you have to cover fixed costs in additional to marginal cost. Your hope is that demand for your good will rise allowing you to increase your price to cover both marginal cost and average cost. Here's the good news: as a firm grows, its average cost falls. If you produce one paperclip, that paperclip is pretty expensive, considering how much it costs to set up everything you need to do it. If you produce 100M boxes of paperclips, the cost per unit falls. This process is known as Economies of Scale.

A simple example of cost concepts might help.

Suppose widgets are produced with a combination of fixed costs (a factory) and variable costs (labor, electricity, raw materials, etc.). Fixed costs don't change as you increase your output, only variable costs rise. And in a basic production process, variable costs rise at an increasing rate because of diminishing Marginal Product of Labor.

Let's look at a chart:

Table 6.1:   Cost of producing widgets

No. of widgets	Fixed cost	Variable cost	Total cost	Marginal cost	Average cost
1	1000	100	1100	—	1100
2	1000	250	1250	150	625
3	1000	500	1500	250	500
4	1000	1000	2000	500	500
5	1000	2000	3000	1000	600
6	1000	5000	6000	2000	1000

When we plot these numbers into a graph, we get something like Figure 6.1:

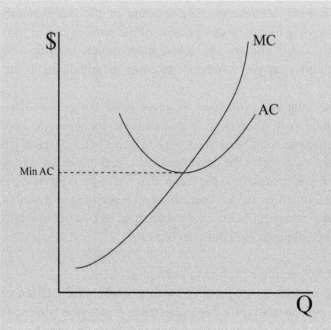

Figure 6.1:   Minimum average cost of producing widgets

In the short run, my widget company could produce three units at a price of 250 because that production covers the cost of the last unit (price = marginal cost), but it doesn't cover average cost; my company is going to lose money this year. The hope is that demand will increase, allowing me to sell more units at a higher price (four units at a price of 500 or five units at a price of 1000), both of which would cover both marginal and average cost.

When a company has a sudden increase in business, it does get closer to achieving long-run viability. Based on this, we assume that all of the business that boomed during Covid should continue to be successful, right? Not exactly. A sudden increase in business that moves the company into a place where it can cover its costs is necessary for long-term success, but not sufficient. The assumption: the increase in demand is permanent. If, as is the case with a lot of Covid changes, the spike in sales is temporary, both average cost savings and price increases will go away in the long run.

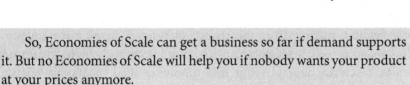

So, Economies of Scale can get a business so far if demand supports it. But no Economies of Scale will help you if nobody wants your product at your prices anymore.

So, what did the pandemic do to change products and prices that might continue in the long run? Well, we know shopping became more difficult, more costly, and riskier during lockdowns, and we know that some in-person shopping patterns have endured for the past two years. How might this have helped firms and what does it mean for their future?

There are a couple of products/companies/innovations that got a whiff of success during the Covid lockdown, but they do not appear to be poised for long-term success. We classify these firms as lucky: they were briefly saved by changing consumer preferences, but market activity means their success might be short-lived. Let's look at two: Peloton and Blue Apron.

As we mentioned in Chapter 2, Peloton was the at-home exercise company that some people turned to when all of the fitness centers and gyms closed. Peloton makes exercise equipment like treadmills and stationary bikes that have big computer screens built in so that you can enjoy the motivation of training with others from the safety of your own home. Great benefit drivers for those wishing to work out and avoid a contagious disease. All in all, machine and subscription with Peloton can cost several thousand dollars.

In the first year of the pandemic, Peloton's revenue increased fourfold. The publicly traded firm went from a valuation of about $1 billion to $4 billion, and its stock price rose from about $30 per share to over $160 at the end of 2020 alone. By January 2022, its stock price was back to $30 per share. Peloton was lucky, and we think we know why.

Pre-Covid, Peloton was pegged as a 'boutique' exercise company, which inherently meant it had limited mass appeal. There are many other at-home exercise equipment competitors, like Nordic Track, which has been around for about 50 years. In the same time period, companies like Orange Theory and Planet Fitness reignited the public's desire for in-person group training in another type of boutique setting. When all of the in-person exercise alternatives disappeared, enthusiasts who had adopted Orange Theory and Planet Fitness approach would, logically, embrace the offerings of a Peloton. Judging from the change in Peloton's stock price, investors thought so as well. But Peloton's price point is extremely high, and it turns out that exercise apps for your smartphone or iPad (including Peloton's own individual app) provide the same benefits at a fraction of the cost of equipment and a subscription. In addition, there weren't any barriers to imitation that prevented Nordic Track from simply putting a large computer screen with workout videos on their own treadmills, rowers, and stationary bikes. The competition entered the market quickly, extreme profits faded, and Peloton is back to where it started.

Keep in mind, though, that Peloton is not gone. It could be argued that the pandemic gave the company a second chance to prove its concept, and not all who adopted it are quick to abandon it. The good news for a company like this is it learned something about its product and the market. The question is: can Peloton do anything with that information? If our earlier suggestion is correct and people prefer doing their workouts in-person, with other people, if that human component is important to the motivation one needs to "get a good workout," then Peloton might not have any long-run mass appeal.

A similar story can be told about Blue Apron. Blue Apron is a meal kit delivery service. Investors were a bit skeptical about the long-term success of this company from its start. Blue Apron first went public in June 2017 at a price of $10 per share, and that price fell steadily to less than $3 per share by early 2020. Covid and the inability of people to shop or go to restaurants boosted sales during that year and the company's stock price increased to about $12 per share within a few months.

Into the latter part of 2020, however, customers began to ask difficult questions about Blue Apron's products, like "what part of my dinner did you really help me with?" In this case, the company's benefit drivers are shopping and portioning. It turns out that, while shopping was still risky and inconvenient, it also included the ability to control the quality of ingredients. Portion control is difficult to do correctly for the mass market. Yes, these services have value in saving time, but to what extent? Could Blue Apron accurately judge the long-term demand for its services at its price point?

All time-saving innovations end up having the same calculation to determine success: is what you're charging me worth the value of the time you're saving me? Many of the home-delivered meal companies were struggling pre-Covid. The price they charged was often perceived as higher than the value of the time saved. Covid allowed them to add a benefit driver: we'll save you time and eliminate the risk of going out. Once consumer perception of the latter risk eased up, the company was faced with decline as customers returned to the store.

People refer to the brief success of firms like Peloton and Blue Apron as a bump, in this case, a Covid Bump. Like Peloton, it remains to be seen what Blue Apron will do with the information is has gained through this time. The company tried to expand by offering a free test drive, which we'll talk about in Chapter 9. Blue Apron offered new customers the first box free. It's saying something that this offer did not create much traction for its products in the long run.

In The News: Housing Prices Go Through the Roof During Covid

During your average recession or depression, asset prices, including home prices, fall rather dramatically. At the beginning of the Covid lockdowns,

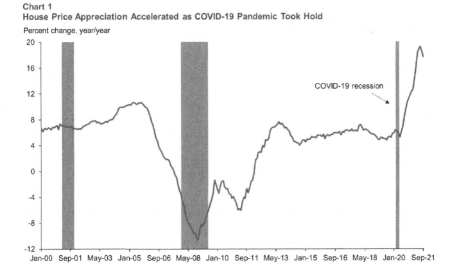

Chart 1
House Price Appreciation Accelerated as COVID-19 Pandemic Took Hold
Percent change, year/year

Figure 6.2: House price appreciation

Notes: The percent change is calculated using the Federal Housing Finance Agency (FHFA) seasonally adjusted purchase-only house price index. Gray bars indicate recessions.
Sources: FHFA; National Bureau of Economic Research.

that happened to stock prices and home prices in the US but both recovered thanks to a combination of government policies and Covid vaccines. Home prices did more than just recover; they skyrocketed across the US. But what caused this dramatic increase? Is the housing market lucky, or good?

Covid's economic impacts have been far reaching and unique. The impacts on the housing market are unusual; but are they permanent? There was an increase in demand as people fled crowded apartment buildings in crowded urban centers for more spacious homes in less crowded suburbs. There was an increase in demand from people who now work from home and wanted or needed more room (like a home office.) Those changes are not likely to reverse anytime soon.

Then there's the impact of government policy. In the US and in many countries, the central bank (the Federal Reserve) pushes interest rates to historic lows. The way that's actually accomplished is for the central bank to buy financial assets like government bonds and, in the US, mortgage-backed securities. The Federal Reserve purchased over $1 trillion worth of mortgages during the pandemic. Whatever impact that policy had on home prices is best described as lucky, or at least limited to the short run.

The Federal Reserve is not in the business of investing in any private enterprise including housing, so at some point they will have to sell these mortgaged-backed securities and when that happens we'll see how much of the home price boom is lucky and how much is good.

Mini Case: Moderna

Recalling the title of this chapter, it isn't entirely fair to call Moderna lucky or good. Unlike Pfizer, Johnson and Johnson, and many of the other Covid vaccine makers, Moderna was not a well-known pharmaceutical company before Covid.

Founded in 2010, Moderna specializes in mRNA products including vaccines. Before Covid, it had never had a commercially successful (or even FDA approved) product although it has been attempting to develop vaccines and therapies for diseases ranging from influenza to HIV to various cancers. mRNA therapies themselves have only been applied to humans since the early 2000s, so that they have not had a successful product is not surprising given the normal development time for new pharmaceutical technologies.

Like all developmental pharma companies, Moderna always struggled to find funding for their research project. It is well known that there are very large upfront costs involved in the process of developing and getting approval for new therapies, hundreds of millions of dollars at least. Moderna went through several rounds of venture financing during its early years before it finally went public in 2018, raising over $600 million with its public stock offering. But the company had lost (spent) $1.5 billion by the end of 2019 without a successful product to show for it.

The search for Covid vaccines and the funding that was made available sparked Moderna and other pharma teams to move faster than before. But the sheer magnitude of the funding infusion for Moderna was notable. Moderna received about a billion dollars for Covid vaccine development and has gotten several billion dollars more from selling the vaccine.

Considering where Moderna was financially and in terms of potentially viable products pre-Covid, and considering the amount of money that was given to them to expedite development of the Covid vaccine, this is a unique case for the question of lucky vs. good. Investigate Moderna's earnings history (EPS) as well as their cash on hand. Does it look as if they will have trouble finding funding for future research projects? Aside from operational needs, what financial prerogative could reduce their stockpile of cash?

Let's assume Covid vaccines will be needed for the foreseeable future. What's the one most important determinant of Moderna's future Covid-based financial success? Investigate the potential for mRNA therapies and treatments. Given that and Moderna's newfound cash hoard, why might you consider them both lucky and good.

Discussion Questions

6.1 Arguably, there was skepticism about Blue Apron and other "meal kit" companies right from the start, but they did have some success and

Covid showed that the concept itself does have demand. Understanding that competitors can enter the market easily, who might provide viable "meal kit" home delivered services in the future?

6.2 Looking at its stock price, Zoom.com would appear to fit into this chapter. Discuss the competitive environment that Zoom has faced more or less since they came into existence a decade ago. How did this change over the Covid timeline?

6.3 Demand for bidets and bidet attachments to traditional toilets soared when toilet paper was in short supply. All things considered, will this represent a long-term trend for that industry?

6.4 Sales of printed books increased dramatically during the pandemic. Why did people buy more books and is this likely to represent a permanent increase for this product sector?

6.5 In the later lockdown phases, researchers predicted a Covid Baby Boom in early 2021. By all accounts, that did not happen. Why not?

7

Right Place, Right Time

"Oh… One More Thing… ."
— *Famous Steve Jobs teaser at the end of many new Apple Keynote presentations*

Throughout this book, we've mentioned some companies and products that benefited from the challenges presented by COVID-19 and some that were hurt. When corporate leadership develops a strategic plan, they rarely include "pandemic preparations," although some might try to make their company more flexible and adaptable to change. Still, as we discussed in the last chapter, some firms were lucky and saw short-term benefits. Others were good and are seeing enduring profits. But there's a third category, where some firms saw opportunity strike exactly when they needed it to. These firms were in the right place at the right time to fill a need created by an unforeseen shock to the system.

We have noted that the pandemic may have accelerated trends already underway in the market. Before March 2020, bricks-and-mortar retail stores and neighborhood malls were already struggling to survive in a shopping world that had gone online. Movie theaters were already dealing with the impact of big-screen TVs and the proliferation of streaming services. Work-from-home, online education, and other remote capabilities were gaining acceptance many years before we were all forced to use them. Tel-a-doc, virtual doctors' visits were already a thing under many insurance plans.

Why does this matter? Well, even if we think of a business lifecycle as clear-cut (you invent something, you bring it to market, and you immediately gauge your success or failure), the truth is that most business innovations take time. A lot of time. What a firm put in place a decade ago may just now be turning profitable. Firms try to estimate future demand to meet it... well... in the future. They do this to avoid the alternative: being behind the curve and unprepared to meet the new trends. Firms pay a lot of money to educate their guesses, but there is still a level of unpredictability in what consumers will want a year, two years, five years from now. So, some firms that have been able to successfully navigate the Covid pandemic are doing so because they developed what they needed to be successful years before it hit. No, we are not suggesting a conspiracy or master plan. We simply propose that these firms, with their established infrastructures, tested services and products, and adaptive supply chains, are in the right place at the right time.

The most visible industries to observe right place/right time are retail, which we all know and love, tech, and entertainment. It's especially helpful that these three industries are virtually indistinguishable from each other in the current economy (Apple and Amazon are tech *and* entertainment firms, after all).

A few examples from this sector include:

Amazon:
Amazon had been speeding up deliveries and expanding offerings into more and "fresher" things for decades. In fact, optimizing its supply chain to deliver more things faster to more locations is part of its very mission.

Apple:
Apple had been expanding its product line to include less-expensive smartphones in an effort to engage all ages and demographics, and the company's easy interface — a pillar of its design aesthetic — has always made it a popular choice among non-tech-savvy consumers.

Starbucks:
Starbucks, which has gone through many expansion and retrenchment initiatives over its lifetime, began experimenting with drive-through service fifteen years ago, its payment app ten years ago, and it had already formed partnerships with early delivery services like GrubHub and UberEats in major markets.

Costco & Target:
Costco and Target both greatly expanded online interfaces, as well as local delivery, fresh-food delivery, and drive-up service in key areas.

Disney:
Disney, whose hospitality and entertainment divisions took a hit during the early lockdown phases, enjoyed one beacon of hope in its Covid journey: the Disney+ streaming service launched on November 12, 2019, a full two months before the first confirmed case of Covid in the United States.

When we look at Covid as a shock to the system, we can characterize firms as winners and losers, good or lucky, short-term opportunists or long-term adapters. But, when we consider the reality that Covid was, in part, an accelerator for existing trends in the marketplace, we can delve deeper and identify a few firms that had prepared, unwittingly, for success. Let's delve deeper into these examples.

Apple, Inc.: A Focus on Accessibility

We've discussed Apple several times already; that's no coincidence. During Covid, Apple became the first company with a market value of $3 trillion. It was already a very successful company, but it continued to thrive without faltering through 2020 and 2021, even into 2022. Why? Accessibility.

Apple's built-in iPhone services, like Facetime, work best with other iPhones. We all know that one family member who makes the group text go green — and we pressure them to get on board, right? All of a sudden, Covid-Christmases required grandma and grandpa to have a phone that can easily interface with all of the grandkids, that's easy to use, and that won't break the bank more than other brands. Enter iPhone: easy to set up, easy to use, and works with everyone in the family.

For a public now acutely aware of health indicators, Apple was ready to help, too. The iWatch had been moving toward more health-based applications, like real-time EKG, pulse oximeter, and activity tracking, for a decade. Add to this an easy interface and quick setup, plus integration with your local doctor's tele-health calling system, and the iWatch becomes a valuable tool for everyone, not just athletes.

And the list continues… need to work from home and take a private call? Apple's Air Pods can help with that. Even Apple's fledgling TV service, like all streaming services, benefited during lockdown — but got a big boost from having some of the most popular offerings available. Original content, like Ted Lasso or The Morning Show, takes years to develop. Apple had these at the ready.

All of these product innovations, decades in the making, would be for nothing if not for Apple's foresight in one other area: supply chain. First, long before the pandemic, Apple began researching the cost–benefit of producing their own chips. Bringing this major component in-house means streamlining its supply chain and accelerating delivery schedules (it also represented a major cost savings in the long run). Second, with a nod toward sustainable practices, the company had been phasing out the provision of additional headphones and other accessories with each new phone. This saved on shipping costs and reduced shipping times further. Finally, as early as 2009, Apple began adjusting its accounting basis away from the iPhone product line into a more general set of products and services. This meant that it limited its exposure to one single product in favor of its expanded product line, including Apple TV streaming services. For a world that would lock down, prioritize health metrics, and stay indoors, Apple products and services were ready.

Amazon.com: A Focus on Proliferation

Amazon is, and always has been, a supply chain company. Its mission has been to optimize delivery of *everything* — from physical goods and marketplace services to streamed content and virtual services. Amazon had been working on one-day and same-day delivery for about a decade before launching in April 2019, a few months before Covid hit. Similarly, it had been developing the infrastructure to deliver products itself, rather than depend on established providers FedEx, UPS, and the USPS. By bringing this critical component of its business in-house, the company now controlled coordination, lowered costs, and offered speedier delivery to its customers. Amazon also acquired Whole Foods in 2017, opening the doors to fresh-food delivery in markets around the world.

Arguably, Amazon's retail business was perfectly positioned for the disruptions in shopping that Covid caused. Click, order, answer the door, done. But that wasn't where most of its profits came from over the past few years. In fact, the fastest growing service provided by Amazon has nothing to do with bringing groceries to your door at all. It's Amazon Web Services. AWS provides the technical internet backbone for some of the largest internet-based companies in the world. Among its largest clients: Netflix, Facebook, LinkedIn, and Twitter. There are dozens of firms each paying tens of millions of dollars a month to keep their online presence up and running. Of course, AWS's biggest growth period came when their business was first beginning to dominate the space, but even during 2020– 2021, AWS's revenue grew by almost 30% annually.

Amazon's success during the pandemic was decades in the making and is attributed largely to the company's focus on convenience. Convenience, in this case, results from the company's proliferation across multiple platforms and supply chain metrics — and this does not happen overnight. Indeed, since its founding, Amazon had been preparing for a level and type of demand like that experienced during the pandemic.

Target: A Focus on Reliability

In 2003, Target made the rather controversial decision (at the time) to allocate a substantial amount of its in-store floorplan to groceries. The move was meant to counter Walmart's strategy to become a "one-stop shop" for all household goods. For both chains, the move to include groceries was a response to Amazon, which had an inventory-based cost advantage for most non-experiential, non-impulse goods. The thought process went something like this: people are moving to Amazon to buy household staples, but they're still shopping for fresh goods in-store themselves. If we offer groceries in our stores, people will come back and buy everything here at the same time. Once they're in our stores, people are more likely to buy other things.

Catering to a somewhat different demographic than Walmart, Target aligned itself with home goods and clothing designers and created a range of store brands that were both high quality and lower cost. It engaged in a series of nationwide store remodels to renovate the existing cafes and add Starbucks to the in-store experience. Understanding that a high percentage of sales came from the impulse buyer, a concept borrowed from K-mart decades earlier, Target also upgraded the in-store music selection and brought on associates dedicated to the technology and electronics department. It also beefed up its online shopping experience, integrating the RedCard rewards program with the app, improving real-time inventory tracking, and simplifying the online ordering and pickup process.

When the lockdown hit, local Target stores had already established a reputation of being customer focused and indeed, one-stop shops. Target had a relatively easy time transitioning into contactless services, including drive-up and pick-up, and it simply expanded its partnerships with Shipt (which Target acquired in 2017, another pre-Covid move that worked out well for them) and Instacart to reach a broader customer base looking for home-delivered convenience. Target had intended to become a reliable retailer, promising convenience and quality superior to Amazon, Walmart, and the neighborhood grocer. It invested in multiple programs designed to enhance its reliability, programs that were a decade or more in development. This dedication to reliability proved successful. Drive-up service in Q-4 2020 increased by 500% (yes, 500%) over the prior year. All same-day services, including drive-up, in-store pick-up, and Shipt's same-day delivery increased by 200% over the year.

The story continued even in the store. Over the prior decade, Target had expanded its use of self-checkout lines. Prior to the pandemic, critics decried this as limiting the "friendly cashier" experience. In March 2020, it was an option for those needing to go to a store but wanting decreased contact with cashiers and a speedier checkout process.

Costco: A Focus on... Focus

When we talk about pandemic successes, right place/right time, we do not mean those who simply benefitted from an uptick in demand. Recalling the prior chapter, those firms are simply lucky, and we expect this luck to fade over time. So, we do not discuss Costco here simply because its stores had long lines of people hoarding household staples. Among retailers, Costco was a Covid success because of its focus, and this was a strategy ingrained in the firm since its inception.

In February 2020, the NASDAQ retail sector declined by about 40%, which was to be expected as investor uncertainty skyrocketed. In the same period, though, Costco's stock fell only 15%. From that low, over the past two years, its stock price has nearly doubled. Aside from great rotisserie chicken and abundant toilet paper, what's so great about Costco?

First, bulk purchasing (shortages notwithstanding) was the fastest, easiest way to stock-up and hoard. While it did have outages of things like brand name toilet paper, Costco's house brand, Kirkland, was available more often than Target's Up-and-Up and other store brands. Why? Costco only carries two brands of toilet paper: Charmin, a P&G brand, and their own Kirkland Signature. Why? By providing fewer choices at bulk purchases, Costco can become a dominant vendor in the market. So what? Well, that increases the company's buying power on products like these, allowing it to negotiate lower prices *and* become a high priority delivery for the producer. The result: Costco only had one brand of toilet paper available, but it was available.

Costco's focus also extended to its accessibility, which was limited by its membership model. No card, no entry, which means each store could more accurately predict demand spikes during the lockdown. Access control is key in preserving the integrity of inventory, and Costco's model proved one of the best in avoiding shortages (more than competitors). It also allowed the company to provide tailored services valued during the pandemic, like senior-citizen shopping hours, which were available to local grocery stores as well but harder to implement in the Targets of the world.

There were a few downsides for Costco. During lockdown, it had to close its famous food court and gasoline sales declined as driving slowed (haha). Here's the fun part: Costco doesn't make money on most of those sales anyway. $5 rotisserie chickens, $1.50 hot dogs, and $0.50 drinks are what we consider "loss leaders" designed to get people into the store. Costco was able to close or limit these offerings and engage in a real-world natural experiment to gauge consumer preference with little hit to its bottom line.

Disney: A Focus on Diversification

When strategists think about an increasingly risky environment, we typically see a market where demand is fluctuating, supply is uncertain, and the competitive environment becomes unclear. Sound familiar? In this case, we recommend some level of diversification to counteract the risk. Similar to playing the stock market, if you diversify the products and services you offer, you limit over-exposing your firm to a host of problems that could occur in one line. Was this strategy effective during Covid? Let's take a look at Disney.

Disney is a large conglomerate, with diverse holdings around the world. It spans the hospitality, entertainment, original content, retail, theme park, and technology sectors — each with their own fluctuations during the pandemic. So, the overall impact of Covid is harder to assess. Let's take the low-hanging fruit: streaming. Disney+ was launched just before the pandemic, featuring a one-of-a-kind catalogue of content for all ages. In addition to classic Disney characters and movies, the platform features Lucasfilm's Star Wars franchise, Marvel Comics' franchise, Disney's own Pirates of the Caribbean franchise, the Pixar catalogue, and much more. Exclusive rights to Star Wars and Marvel were in development years before 2020, and the strategy to keep Disney as the sole provider of all Disney content has been in place since its founding. You can't watch *The Little Mermaid* on Netflix, and you never will. Disney acquired Pixar in 2006, well before the pandemic. With this breadth of content cultivated years before, Disney's streaming service boomed during lockdown and has grown steadily ever since. For this specific product line, entertainment, it was a success.

Other products and services in the Disney portfolio were not so well prepared to capitalize on the pandemic. On the contrary, they suffered. Disney owns ABC and ESPN. Without large-scale sporting events around the world, the networks lost advertising revenue across broadcast and online platforms. For ESPN, this was the continuation of years of declines; indeed, Disney has been called upon multiple times to jettison the ESPN lineup from its holdings. Network TV: bust.

What about hospitality? Because the pandemic affected properties worldwide, Disney Cruise Lines ceased operations temporarily and many Disney hotel properties downsized operations. Hospitality services were not prioritized or favored during the pandemic but are happily recovering now that lockdowns are easing, and tourism is growing once again. The same story is told for Disney's theme park holdings, such as Disneyland, Disney World, and the other properties across the world. If we take stock price as a well-understood metric, the overall effect of Covid on Disney was a wash. The price of Disney stock has remained virtually unchanged pre- and post-pandemic. Comparatively, Six Flags Entertainment is an entertainment/theme park company without streaming services, but with

TV networks. It saw a decline in stock price of about 30% over the course of the pandemic. Although not a resounding success, it would appear that Disney diversified well enough to withstand a major global event that hit many of its sectors at the same time.

Disney would do well to follow the lead of other companies and use this natural experiment to think about changes in its product offerings. It has already become something of a template for other companies in similar industries. Casino gambling — dependent on the face-to-face, experiential model that had sustained it for centuries — suffered considerably in early stages of the pandemic. However, the industry accelerated development of online gaming platforms that helped bolster revenues in the downtime. Like the fans in the stands and people in the gym, some companies were able to compensate for the lack of human interaction, at least in the short term. It will be interesting to see how many people want to gamble this way in the future.

Concept Review: Game Theory, Sequential Games, & Early Mover Advantages

Game theory is an area of study that gives us tools and approaches for solving a very specific set of problems. We are aware that the choices of others, usually perceived as independent players, together with our own choices, determine an outcome.

We use game theory a lot in life. As a matter of fact, we use it all the time. Choices at work, choices in relationships, and choices in sports all use the approaches of game theory. Decisions of all kinds are games. Driving is a game. Shopping is a game (sometimes, a competitive one). Navigating the politics at work can be a game. A game just means you can't determine your outcomes on your own. In the world in which we live, we are hard-pressed to find something we can do that doesn't have any effect on others.

Do you play tennis? Here's a question: why don't you just stand up at the net all the time and swat back the other player's shots? That's easy... the opposing player will hit one over your head. In baseball, why doesn't the pitcher throw fast, straight pitches every time? Because a good baseball player will learn to hit a home run. When you go home to your significant other after a day at work (or, in recent times, when you emerge from the home office), why don't you always plop down in front of the TV and put on your favorite show? Because that's simply not going to work out the way you intended. In every instance, the other player is empowered to make a choice that changes your outcome.

In game theory, we describe two different types of games: simultaneous and sequential. The difference is timing. Simultaneous games are ones were the players make their choices at the same time (or at least without knowing what the other player chose). In these games, each player has to look at the *potential* outcomes and try to determine what their best choice is given all the possible choices that the other player *could* make.

Other games are called sequential (Figure 7.1). Like checkers or chess, you make your choice after the other player chooses. The approach

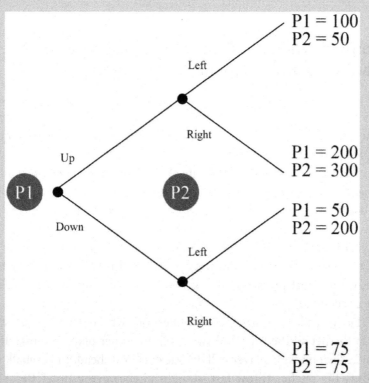

Figure 7.1: A sequential game with two players

one takes in these games is to look ahead and make your choice based on what the other player will do. Generally, you can assume they will make the choice that is best for them.

Consider a basic game with two players, P1 and P2. Each player has to choose which direction to go, and P1 chooses first:

If all of the information is known, P1 would look at all of the possible outcomes and ask which one he could attain knowing P2 will always make her choice in order to maximize her own final number. Put another way: P1 knows P2 will always choose what makes her happy, and he'll back off his choice accordingly. This game works out well for both players. If P1 picks Up, then P2 can only get 50 (if she picks left) or 300 (if she picks right.). P2 will pick right and that gives P1 their best outcome, 200. Sequential games don't have to work out this way, but this one does.

Suppose two firms, The Coca-Cola Company and PepsiCo, are each considering launching a new soda. They could choose to launch a new flavor of soda or a new type of diet soda. When firms think about launching a product, they usually estimate profits based on market studies, historical data, and competitor analysis. All of this information feeds into a ballpark estimate of profits for each firm, which can be shown in a payoff matrix like this (Figure 7.2):

	THE COCA-COLA COMPANY™	
	NEW DIET SODA	NEW FLAVORED SODA
PEPSICO™ NEW DIET SODA	−1 / −4	10 / 6
NEW FLAVORED SODA	7 / 8	0 / −2

Figure 7.2:   Payoffs of the Coca-Cola vs. Pepsi game

If the firms are making their decisions simultaneously, each one's biggest concern is that it might choose the same thing as its competitor. If both release a new flavor, or both release a new diet soda, neither one will profit. One way to restructure the game (in the classroom or in the real world) is to let one of the firms choose first.

Suppose Coke announces its choice first. Then, the decision tree would look like this (Figure 7.3):

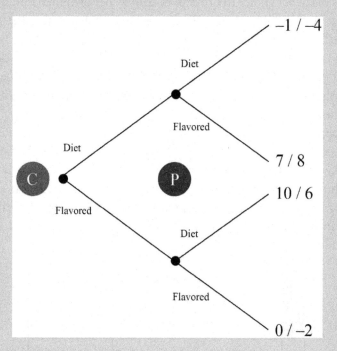

Figure 7.3: Payoffs of a sequential game, Coke chooses first

Coke would pick a new flavored soda, then Pepsi would pick a new diet soda. Coke would get profits of 10 and Pepsi would get profits of 6. Both make profits.

This game has what's called a *first mover advantage*. Coke reaps the benefits of being able to choose its new product first. What if we play it the other way? If we let Pepsi pick first, the game would look like this (Figure 7.4):

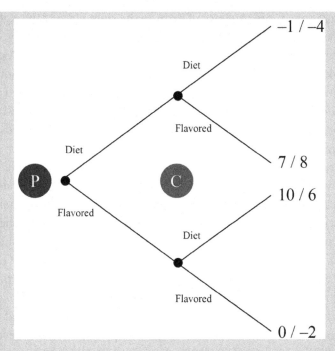

Figure 7.4:   Payoffs of a sequential game, Pepsi chooses first

Pepsi would launch a new flavored soda, Coke would launch a new diet soda; Pepsi would get 8 and Coke would get 7. The results are similar, but now Pepsi has the advantage.

Here's the thing: first-mover advantage sounds great on paper, but it is a lot less certain in the real world. Game theory is supposed to be conceptual, not literal. It is a framework for approaching situations that are similar to the problems that we do in the classroom. But that is all it is: a framework.

We can ascribe certain business successes to an early-mover advantage, like Starbucks's drive-through or Amazon's same-day delivery. We also have to acknowledge that the "early" part of the advantage means these firms began developing these new offerings before the pandemic began. This means these firms were prepared to serve needs they couldn't have imagined would exist years later. Put differently, chance does indeed favor the prepared … firm.

There is one more category of firms in the right place at the right time: established necessities. Quite a few corporations were already serving needs that quickly became major priorities. Clorox, Lysol, GoJo Industries (the maker of Purell and other hand sanitizers), Campbell's Soup, and other shelf-stable food companies — all faced increased need during the pandemic and will likely see a sustained increase in demand for the foreseeable future. These firms were able to anticipate the needs of the Covid world.

There were also a few companies whose offerings, like bidets as an alternative to toilet paper, will see long-term demand simply because they were adopted out of necessity. For each of these companies there were short-term boosts in demand and resulting supply shortages. The ability of a company to get products on the shelf quickly determined the short-run profits from Covid. The ability of a company to accurately estimate demand *moving forward* may dictate whether it continues to see profits in the long run.

The key question for these firms: how durable is the demand created by the forced test drive? For a generation of people that had never tried Campbell's Soup or Chef Boyardee Ravioli or Del Monte canned pears, Covid forced them to. Since there was no time to reformulate the product, demand was based entirely on availability. As the old products return to the shelves, how much will demand for the substitutes change? And bidets? Well, those made a short-term splash (sorry), but the level of permanent adopters is likely to be lower. Not zero, but lower.

Germ-killing wipes, hand sanitizers, and other products in that market will likely see a boost in sales for many years. One thing Covid has done is persuaded the masses that a communicable, airborne, easily transmissible disease that can reach pandemic levels is not some far-fetched, Hollywood idea; it is a very real possibility. We wash our hands more, we need soap more, and demand continues.

By the time you are reading these words, you will know somebody who contracted COVID-19. Sadly, many of us know people who were quite sick and perhaps died. Covid has made hand sanitizer, facial coverings, and contactless transactions a permanent part of life in most countries. Companies whose products — products developed a decade before — coincidentally align with that reality are benefiting from this regime shift.

Interesting Aside

There were a few surprising winners during the Covid era. One that revealed something interesting about human nature was the restaurant chain The Cheesecake Factory. Started as a cheesecake bakery in 1972, the restaurant began expanding its food offerings and became a mainstay dining and bar attraction in the late 1990s. Although its cheesecake varieties were still a draw, they moved to the periphery of the product as The Cheesecake Factory became known for convenient dining, good food, a relaxed atmosphere, and a lively bar scene. Like many other casual dining chains, it saw its overall business decline during the lockdown phase. Ah, but wait. It turns out that lonely, locked-down people needed comfort food. A piece of cheesecake (which packages in to-go boxes and survives delivery very well) fits the bill perfectly. While Cheesecake Factory struggled to sell most of their menu items during Covid, sales of their namesake product — cheesecake — increased!

Mini Case: Starbucks 💡

Starbucks is not a coffee shop. While coffee-flavored beverages are one of its products, that alone could not explain its success. Coffee is too easy to make, too easy to copy, and not at all an original product to bring to market. So, why is it one of the most profitable businesses in the world? Aside from one of our author's addictions to venti chai latte's…

Starbucks' benefit driver began as customer service. At its founding, it was the cornerstone of the company. Starbucks designed its stores to be the 'neighborhood bar' of coffee shops. It's like the TV series *Cheers*: "everybody knows your name," and through the early years, you really could walk into a Starbucks and have your local barista whip up your caramel latte without saying a word.

But volume (increasing per-store sales) and growth (a Starbucks on every corner) made maintaining that neighborhood feel very difficult. How can you know the name of every person who walks through your door in downtown Los Angeles? That's where other benefit drivers come in: consistency (reverse osmosis ensures the same-tasting water is used to brew drinks and make ice *everywhere*), reliability (open at the same time every day), creativity in their product mix (no pun intended), and of course, happy, cheerful customer service even if the barista doesn't know your name.

Starbucks shifted its benefit driver without erasing service completely, allowing it to grow considerably over the past four decades. This strategy also allowed the company to adopt features your neighborhood coffee shop didn't have: drive-through ordering and door-to-door delivery (a latte and a bagel brought right to your door? In 1992, who knew? Now, it's there in 30 minutes or less). Starbucks also continues to enjoy a sense of presence, having expanded into local grocery stores and Target stores across the world. It is now your neighborhood coffee shop wherever you happen to be.

So, how does a ubiquitous coffee shop with standardized — yet copyable — products fare during a pandemic? It turns out, pretty well… because it's not really a coffee shop anymore. Starbucks has been a winner during the pandemic due to its drive-through service and app-based ordering system. These features — developed 15 years before the start of COVID-19 — gave it an enormous jump start on other coffee providers. In a world searching for comfort and normalcy (and also somewhat addicted to coffee), providing a comfort item through relatively safe drive-through or contactless delivery wins.

Even a right place/right time company like Starbucks is not fully protected from the effects of the pandemic, however. Many stores have faced the same challenges as other service-industry counterparts: a shortage of labor, which limits staffing at each location, and supply chain hiccups, that limit supply of major ingredients like sugar, syrups, mix-ins, and milks. Starbucks has moved to incentivize employment and employee retention through one of the most generous recruiting, training, and benefits packages in the industry. It has also reformulated select drink recipes and optimized delivery of limited ingredients regionally. Starbucks did not deal with a spike in demand during Covid; it dealt with a blow to its supply of talent and ingredients. It is a reminder that no company, even those in the right place at the right time, could sail through the pandemic without adapting quickly in some way.

Discussion Questions

7.1 Is it always best to be a first mover? What benefits might exist for second (or third) entrants into a particular market?

7.2 Target has recently announced it will test a program where you can pick up your Starbucks order at the same time you pick up your drive-up order, getting both Target and Starbucks without leaving your car. Why?

7.3 Internet Service Providers. Arguably, their service offerings were in development for half a century before the pandemic hit, and they were in the right place at the right time. What challenges did they face in the early lockdown phases and how might they change moving forward?

7.4 Apple and Amazon are two of the most successful companies in the world based on their market value in 2022. They did and are doing a lot of things right. But high-profile success often brings government intervention. What part of Apple's business (not patent litigation) has already been part of lawsuits? On a separate front, why is Amazon frequently mentioned when regulators mention breaking up tech companies?

7.5 Most of our "right place, right time" companies saw existing strategies accelerate during Covid. Other Covid beneficiaries, like hand sanitizer company Purell, will likely see a small increase in long term demand because of a structural change. What change?

8

If Your Home Is Your Castle, Is It Time to Re-moat?

"The house of every one is to him as his castle and fortress as well for defense against injury and violence as for repose."

— *Sir Edward Coke*

Covid did not start the move toward remote work. It simply sped it up dramatically and suddenly. So, Covid didn't force us to replace in-person communication with email, Microsoft Teams, FaceTime, text messaging, etc. It just made these forms of communication which were peripheral and acceptable for informal communication acceptable for formal (even legal) work-related transactions. Working from home over the past two years, many people have learned something interesting that the pre-Covid remote workers already knew about the convenience of working from home: convenience comes with a big cost. You never get to "go home from work." Work is now with you all the time. And for many people, that means you're actually working more hours and working harder to get things done.

If your home and work environments are one and the same, what do you do? If your home is your castle, do you need to re-moat?

Alright, it's a cute metaphor. But you can see what we mean, right? Back in the day, a castle moat was *literally* a barrier to entry. It had a drawbridge that was opened only for certain people and only at certain times. Never having owned a castle, we're going to guess that it wasn't proper to leave the drawbridge down at night... or after everyone's gone to sleep. Kind of defeats the purpose, really. You can always put the bridge down if a friendly face drops by unexpectedly, but the default after-hours status is protection and no access to you and your castle.

When we work from work, there is a clear separation in work and home environments. Whether you drive, fly, walk, bus, or otherwise commute is irrelevant. There is a definitive moat around your home castle, and your control over the drawbridge is absolute. Working from home… that's a different story. Pulling up the drawbridge isn't as simple as getting in your car. Now, you have to log off *multiple platforms*, maybe set your phone to do-not-disturb, put those files where you can't see them, close all the browser tabs, clear off the kitchen table or couch or bed, and unlock the home office door to let the dog in (or out). You need to blur your Zoom background, so nobody sees the clothes hanging out of the hamper. You need to put a post-It note over your webcam so you can breastfeed your newborn. One drawbridge has turned into many.

Here's the thing: a moat — a real-life bog of water and tadpoles and some kind of seaweed-looking thing — is a clear boundary. You know it's there. Your enemies know it's there. Your friends know it's there. You know your enemies and friends know it's there. As signals go, there's very little to explain about a moat. Stay out unless I let you in. But as work and life spaces became more integrated, we lost the clear-cut moat that indicates when we're "on" and when we are "off." How do you define a boundary when you have to re-define it in multiple places?

To some extent, this is an older issue. Work–life balance has been a popular area of discussion for decades. When it was first bandied about in the latter half of last century, the line between work and life was clearer and cleaner. For most people, work was done at the factory or the office or the store and life was done at home or at the beach or on the ski slopes. The slosh over would be things like "taking your work home with you," not literally in most cases, but emotionally or psychologically. Life could slosh into work too; family issues interfering with work or something similar.

But the work–life balance had pretty clear boundaries back then. Now? Not so much. Ironically, very few things of the coping mechanisms that people came up with for the original work–life balance problems apply to today's version. For many people, work and life have never been so close.

And boundaries are just plain hard to figure out. Is your toddler cute to everyone else in that Zoom meeting? Don't be so sure.

Breaking down boundaries can be useful. Letting people (bosses, team members, assistants, whomever) know you have a life can help with re-establishing your boundaries, but there needs to be a strategy in place. The more haphazard you are with your boundaries, the less you'll end up maintaining effective boundaries. Work–life balance is still a thing; but it's a very different thing and it needs serious reconsideration.

Let's review game theory. When we look at the need for signals, pieces of information that help players know one another, we discuss *commitments*. A commitment is something you have established before the game is played (before a decision is made) that helps frame your way of doing things. In this way, the other player knows something about you and can act accordingly. But there's a catch: to be effective (to change the game), a commitment must be credible. If the other player thinks you'll change your mind for some reason, a commitment is pretty much worthless. Commitments are boundaries, like moats, but they become easier to cross when you're not consistent. Raise your hand if you say you'll never answer your phone after 5:00, but you usually do, and they keep calling you. The moat that you have is one of your own making.

Concept Review: Commitments

Commitments are familiar to all of us. What's less familiar is when one should use them and when they work. A commitment works when it makes the person who makes the commitment better off if they follow through. That is, people will believe you're going to do something if it really will benefit you. In traditional game theory, we say that commitments work best when they are three things: credible, observable, and irreversible. Let's look at a few examples.

Credibility

Suppose you're a free agent/consultant in the IT industry. You're really good at what you do, and you make a lot of money on various contracts for different companies (you always sign a non-disclosure agreement, so no worries there). You work a lot and you enjoy your career. The income is healthy, but unstable, but you balance that with your other benefits of being a consultant and choose to continue being a free agent.

Then, one day, you take on a new client and you love this particular job. The contract is rewarding, plus the people are great and the pay is even better. They like working with you, too, and pretty soon, you're signing a lot of contracts with this company. Eventually, the company offers you a full-time gig for about as much as you're making annually now. You'd be employed full-time, with benefits, at a company you have come to know and love — but you have to commit to them and only them for the foreseeable future.

Your thought process might go something like this:

- I choose to commit to the firm, being gainfully employed at about the same rate I get now, with stable income, benefits, and a work environment I love, but I lose the option to work with other firms that might be even better.
- I choose to continue my work as a consultant, being employed at the same rate, but unpredictably, with no benefits, and working with some people I like, some people I don't. Something as good as this firm might not come along again. Then again, it might.

If you have been in the industry awhile and you know the field, you might consider "settling down" and accepting the offer of exclusivity. Your commitment to the firm would be credible, in that it knows you would make the best choice for you. You make that choice, and the company has no reason to doubt you. You have made a credible choice.

The commitment makes you better off, so it's credible. What about observable?

Observable

Talk is cheap. If you make the commitment to the new company, but you still take contracts on the side, what happens? The company can only come after you for things they know about, right? This is true, and from the company's side, they may not trust you as a former independent contractor-turned-full-time employee if you continue to work from home. So, you offer to come into the office three days a week. Or you start using their laptops and servers, so they can track your workload. *You* have to offer up some sort of observability to increase the credibility of your commitment. "Not only will I work for you, but I will also let you *see* me working for you so you know I'm there."

Companies have formalized measures to enhance observability and remaining loyal to the terms of your employment. It is one of the main reasons some firms resist the permanent move to work-from-home.

Irreversibility

Is there any way to make the commitment irreversible? Sure, companies do this all the time. Exclusivity contracts, punitive NDAs, and other legal avenues disincentivize cheating on your new firm. Social pressures might also keep you from violating your contracts if your reputation and integrity matter to your future. These kinds of things also make the commitment relatively irreversible. Yes, you can quit your job, but it's not as easy as quitting a single contract as a consultant. The nature of this commitment is a sense of permanence and backing away from that has consequences. That you would accept the permanent contact knowing it is more irreversible makes your choice even more credible.

Commitments work to change a game (in this case, your employment prospects), but the devil is very much in the details. Signing on the dotted line is just the start of a nuanced process that helps the commitment serve a larger purpose.

Credibility, observability, and irreversibility greatly impact your work–life balance since they factor into your commitments and boundaries. For those whose work environment has shifted, it also explains some of the (ongoing) strife Covid caused home-workers. But this framework can help provide structure as you re-moat (i.e., re-establish your boundaries). A few guidelines:

1. If you show a willingness to answer some peoples' messages but not others, this will create new problems. In this case, you are fostering

credibility, but with different tribes. Consistency is key. Set boundaries and don't make exceptions. This prevents having an "insiders" vs. "outsiders" problem that complicates your work and life. Even the old "cheats" of using your personal communication channels (personal phone, Gmail, etc.) to communicate more frequently with some people will eventually leak out. And it misses the point of the moat! You need to be off sometimes. Your terms are up to you.

2. Higher-ups in many businesses have known about boundary-setting/work–life balance for years, and in many cases they have set boundaries … for themselves. No work during vacations; no work on Sunday; no work after 10PM and before 6AM; whatever they found that let them get the job done but avoid burnout. Now, they oversee employees who are working from home. The Golden Rule helps here: do unto others as you would have others do unto you. If you want/ need your boundaries respected, you need to respect the boundaries of your employees. They may not be the *same* boundaries, but they are boundaries.

3. In the best interpersonal relationships, reputation is maintained through open communication. Having clear and consistent boundaries can help both employees and employers, since there is no ambiguity, and the boundaries are easily observed and understood.

The Great Resignation, Redux

Commitments and boundaries can also explain the 2021 labor market, where masses of people across all sectors voluntarily left their jobs. Dubbed "The Great Resignation," employers are still trying to reconcile workplace incentives with the inability to retain talent. Why are people leaving when "normal" is returning? The answer: people re-moated in a big way.

Burnout has always been a problem in the workplace, but by all accounts it became pervasive and deeply problematic during the Covid era. The strange new world that everyone experienced in the workplace (and in all aspects of life) ultimately worked out for many businesses. Most employees, however, were tossed onto a learning curve with few safety nets and even fewer guidelines. Comfort zones disappeared. Rules were bent. The prior understanding of boundaries, wherever they were, was rendered useless. Many of the parameters that made a workforce successful, like standardized training, in-person management, and team building, became impossible and irrelevant.

During the pandemic, productivity has come at a much higher price — even if labor was allowed to work from home. And very few companies understood that. Bosses had an unfortunate tendency to believe that the new work situation was a lot less stressful because employees could work more flexibly in the "comfort" of their home. They did not consider all of the new stressors that this new work environment created. Furthermore, employees who could not leave the workplace, like healthcare workers, essential workers, sanitation workers, and a host of others, were met with a brand-new set of challenges. Irate customers, tense environments, looming illness, unpredictable supply chains, and a general sense of unease don't make for a fun working environment.

What happened? Well, people re-moated.

Let's define the "old normal" as business-as-usual prior to 2020. On the spectrum of exceptional boundaries to zero boundaries, it's neutral. People were pushed to accommodate a lot of things during the pandemic, pushing their boundaries closer to zero. They compromised, forgave, and had to be flexible on a number of things that weren't even issues before, like abusive patients and customers, long work hours, and even working without pay. Over the course of the pandemic, though, people began re-evaluating boundaries. Some redefined their boundaries *past* that neutral point. The pendulum swung the other way. The labor force sent a clear message: the new normal was not a good way to do things, and neither was the old normal. They re-moated closer to home and decided not to budge on their boundaries — boundaries that were credible, observable, and at least to a point, irreversible.

Did lack-of-boundary work environments cause The Great Resignation on their own? No, but it's not difficult to see that the pandemic adjusted priorities for all of us. Wanting a safer shopping experience and wanting a safer working experience are driven by the same need. All of a sudden, the pool table in the break room isn't enough to those who have re-moated in their work–life experience.

Part of the problem with discussing work environments is the myriad factors that come into the issue. The Great Resignation made headlines because of aggregate numbers, but many industries have clearly been hit harder than others — and many more challenges are to come. Any research into this topic must home in on the effects of demographics, age, income, opportunities, education, job availability, culture, hazards, and the list goes on and on. In aggregation, we lose the human concerns that are at the root of all of this. In aggregation, we miss the point.

Interesting Aside

A big winner during the Covid era has been the home improvement industry. Home Depot's stock price doubled and Lowe's stock price almost tripled between March 2020 and December 2021. Even luxury home improvements like swimming pool installations saw dramatic increases in the last year. This is not hard to explain: people are spending more time at home. When you don't spend money outside, you fluff the nest inside. Your home is your castle, but more and more, it's where you spend much of your time. Maybe in addition to a re-moat, you also need to renovate.

Mini Case: Ulta Beauty, Inc.

Ulta Beauty Inc. is the largest cosmetics chain in the US. It carries a wide variety of products that usually fall under the category of beauty products. Of all the surprising winners during Covid, Ulta would have to be the one that, initially, makes no sense. After all, you don't need lipstick if you're wearing a mask. But the numbers don't lie. Since the decline it experienced when lockdowns began in March 2020 until last Christmas, Ulta's stock price has very nearly tripled.

At first blush (you'll pardon the pun), you would think the make-up industry would be decimated by changes we all experienced: work from home, masks when you shopped at stores, bars and restaurants closed or limited capacity. None of this would dictate the need for more beauty products. But as the expression goes, the camera doesn't lie and suddenly everyone is on camera!

There's a trick part to this market. Camera make-up isn't necessarily the same as in person make-up. And getting that right is different for everyone. Enter Ulta's Glamlab virtual make-up advisor app. Launched in 2016, Glamlab lets users find the perfect products for every occasion and, of course, let's you get said products at Ulta.

Covid, arguably, was just what the doctor ordered for Ulta and Glamlab. How did the confluence of on-camera work-from-home changes, lockdowns, and the fledgling Glamlab's app all come together to make Ulta a Covid winner? Given the concept of early mover advantages and the somewhat forced test drive many people had with the app, will Ulta's Covid success be limited to the short run or more long lasting? What are the biggest threats to its long run success? Are there things Ulta and Glamlab can do to mitigate these threats?

Discussion Questions

8.1 In the modern, blended workplace, there is a tendency to forget boundaries and expect work or at least interaction at all hours of the day. If people aren't punching the clock anymore, they certainly *could* be working at hours other than "nine to five." Suggest a corporate policy that could address these modern realities (e.g., work windows?).

8.2 If the policy you suggested in Question 1 were put into place, how could the employer make it a *commitment* as opposed to a *suggestion*? Is this possible in the long-term?

8.3 Why have some firms resisted the permanent move to work-from-home? What about being in the office enhances credibility for workers? For the firm?

8.4 In theory, work-limit rules could come from either employers or employees, but realistically, employer-determined rules are much more likely to work. Why?

8.5 Healthcare workers continue to face massive burnout and recruitment/ retention are at all-time lows. Yet, Health Sciences and Medical Education remain the most popular training programs (think nursing, pre-med, etc...) in the United States. Why?

9

Marketing with a Mask

"Bet you can't eat just one.™"
— *Lay's Potato Chips*

Marketing is many things in the business world. It is the establishment of a brand name that gives customers product expectations. It is the announcement of change and information about attributes in things like new models of cars or smartphones. It is the source of information about new products, including potential substitutes for things we already use. It is research into trends that could/should happen in the future. If you have a market, anything you do in/to/with it involves Marketing.

Marketing is a catch-all for a lot of sub-disciplines like research, product testing, promotions, data analytics, and the most visible one: advertising. Ultimately, Marketing is just product-oriented storytelling. Sometimes, it tries to convince you to buy, invest, or otherwise jump on the bandwagon for a particular product, service, technology, or company. Other times, it tries to convince you *not* to do these things. From multi-channel to multi-level, marketing is part art, part business designed to turn consumers into customers at every level.

Marketing is taken for granted. A lot. Commercials and billboards and popup ads whiz by us so often that we don't notice them (which sort of missed the point). We're immune to many forms of guerrilla marketing on social media, where "word of mouth" has taken on a new definition. Marketing has been called the "sinister function of business," in that it subversively tries to sway people toward a purchase, whether they can afford it or not.

Yet, without marketing, even the best products or most established brands would wither and die. Open a restaurant and have it become the absolute best restaurant in a hundred-mile radius. Fantastic food, great service, gorgeous ambiance — it should be a success on its own, right? Nope. No marketing, no customers. With all your glowing attributes, you're not going to succeed. You don't know your market, and without marketing, it most assuredly doesn't know you.

Marketing takes many forms and has experienced many changes in the past 20 years. The rise of social media of all forms, cord-cutting and the move to commercial-free streaming, the prevalence (and reliance on) big data, and the general *speed* at which the world now moves have impacted the definition of the word "campaign." Ask two marketers in two different industries what they do, and you'll get two very different job descriptions. Individual consumer targets have risen over the aggregated masses, and pricing, payment, medium, and message are no longer the only ways to appeal to them. Don Draper's catchy tag lines no longer fit the diffuse, randomly sourced world of modern marketing.

But one thing has remained constant: people need stuff and things. No matter the industry or market sector, if you have a *market*, you have a customer. Sure, the advent of the Internet has changed our demand for many things. Technological advances have supplanted some company products and services and given rise to others. This is just industrial evolution. But as long as there is a need to connect what a company is selling with a buyer, there will be a need for Marketing. For suppliers, sellers, and producers, there are always stories to tailor, bits of information to research, ideas to test, and relationships to build.

This last point is key: relationships. Marketing is selling a type of connection to a product or service — and it's the product or service that dictates how this relationship should go. Some things lend themselves to word-of-mouth and can be bought from a distance. For other things, we like to try before we buy. (Arguably, that has changed over the years, too. Return windows and free shipping are better than they were a decade ago. Now, let's just say we would like to try before we're *stuck* with it.) The bottom line is, no matter the prevalence of technology or the reliability of user ratings, we humans like to know how something really feels. To do that, you need a test drive.

Concept Review: Substitutes and the Test Drive

Substitutes, a cornerstone of the Demand Side of the market model, become substitutes once we become aware of their existence and the extent of their substitutability. If that sounds a bit circular (and redundant), think about the consumer's problem. Consumers make purchases to maximize their happiness or, as we discussed in Chapter 1, maximize their utility. But nothing about this process is automatic or innate. We learn how to do this. With the possible exception of breastmilk, humans are not pre-wired with a taste or desire for any goods. We are taught about preferences early in life and we learn how to figure out what we like. That is, we learn how to sample things.

This sampling process is critical to the introduction of new products into the marketplace. Taste tests, free samples, and literal test drives are part of a learning mechanism that allow new products to become substitutes. We know that this process, which we will generically call the test drive, works well for some goods and not for others.

Consider two major household purchases: a big, new flat-screen TV and a new washing machine. Go to almost any store that's selling both of them (Costco) and you'll see the same thing. The TVs are all turned on, often to the same program, side by side. Why? Customers are being allowed to test drive the TVs. You can look at whatever attributes matter to you — price, color quality, sound, refresh rate, thinness, durability, smart features, etc. — and compare. Customers will use the test drive, perhaps with some online reviews of quality, to make a purchase.

Now, wander over to the washing machines and appliances. They are hooked up to electricity and you can see the flashing lights, but you can't put a load of dirty clothes in and see how well it works. Washing machines, by the nature of the product, can't be test driven. For these, customers will use things like reputation or reviews — or maybe just ask someone they know. Based on reviews from sources *they* trust, they will make a purchase.

Test drives are a very useful way for consumers to get first-hand knowledge of a product's attributes and qualities, but the type of test drive that is most effective varies from product to product. "Test drive-ability" is in the nature of the product itself. Any product you can give people a sample of, whether in the store, in the mail, or as a freebie when buying something else, is easy to test drive. But, it also has to be something consumers will use soon enough to *remember* what they thought about it. Lightbulbs are oddly difficult to give away as free samples. They break easily (so mail or the Sunday paper won't work), and by the time you use it at home, you'll probably forget where it came from.

Samples are also not free to the producer. This is probably why we usually don't see anyone giving away free jars of caviar on a Saturday grocery store trip. If you go to a winery for a tasting, they won't usually open their most expensive bottle for you to taste. Once it's open, the vineyard can't sell it, and it doesn't want to throw away the rest of a great bottle.

On the other hand, as any Sunday trip to Costco will reveal, some products are easy to test drive. Free samples of the chicken salad? Check. The latest gluten-free pancakes? Check. Energy drink? Check. Time your day right, and you can get a decent brunch while walking the aisles. You can purchase these items right next to the sample table, packaged and ready to go. No need to wait for a shipment or experience buyer's remorse. The product is available, and the deal can close immediately.

With instant testing, evaluation, and purchase, the test drive is beneficial to the producer, too. Vendors showcasing products at Costco can see exactly which samples were successful in real time and adjust the next day's strategy. They can also feed information back to central marketing departments who can aggregate information across multiple platforms. Test drives are not always perfect — and they can even be deceptive. What's good in a sample size may not be something you want in bulk (do you really need a five-pound carton of dried parsley?). Some test drives are not indicative of the product overall. Still, regardless of whether you end up buying a product or service, test drives remain a popular way to learn about new products.

Test drives have two stages: (1) experiencing the product/service and (2) forming an opinion about whether it is a substitute for your favorite choice. Stage 3 — whether it becomes your *new* favorite — will take more time, but the test drive provides the consumer with an immediate assessment and is at least actionable. That is, a test drive allows a consumer to decide to buy or not to buy.

So, what happened during Covid? While person-to-person interactions became limited, "easy" test drives like snack samples or free movies (or free classes) took a hit. On the other hand, a lack of information early in the pandemic led many to panic and stockpile goods, leading to shortages on everything from toilet paper to baking powder. This caused an increase in test driving, as consumers were forced to try new brands (many of them unknown), since their old favorites were unavailable. For consumers, lockdown panic during Covid led to a massive, forced test drive of thousands of goods and services.

For producers, Covid also led to a forced test drive of new production and distribution methods. Border closures and increased screening measures strained supply chains already at maximum capacity. All of a sudden, new methods of production and distribution were necessary. Many firms adapted, changing ingredients, limiting production of certain flavors/types in favor of more popular ones, and rationing distribution across different locations.

Test drives for consumers and producers happened at the same time — and with little warning. As we have discussed in prior chapters, some firms were able to respond to the rapid changes, some were lucky, and some were in the right place at the right time to capitalize on long-term trends. Today, in the endemic side of the plight, both groups are learning the results of these tests: what worked, what didn't, what needs to stick around, what needs to go back to normal or change again in the future. The forced test drive has valuable information on which all individuals in an economy can act.

The critical impact of Covid's forced test drives was on the market demand for many goods and what we think of as knowledge about *substitutes*. When we talk about substitutes in economics, we talk in terms of demand curves — specifically, the steepness of a demand curve. A good that has only a few (known) substitutes has a steeper curve than something with a lot of substitutes. Why? Well, if there aren't any substitutes, the quantity doesn't change much when price changes, because there aren't as many choices. Think about water: virtually every beverage (soda, beer, milk, juice) is made of water. If the price changes a little, chances are you won't change your consumption. Same goes for gas (remember, we're talking about relative consumption), as well as addictive goods like cigarettes (its why governments know they can impose hefty taxes on them). Strictly speaking, when we refer to a steep demand curve, we say it is *inelastic*, meaning a change in price doesn't usually cause a big change in demand.

When a good has lots of substitutes, its demand is flatter (Figure 9.1). We call this an *elastic* demand curve, meaning demand changes a lot when the price changes. If the price of apples (and only apples) rises, people can switch to pears or peaches or bananas or kiwi or guava or ... well, you get the picture. Think about bottled water: if the price of Dasani suddenly triples, and a case of Aquafina is still $5.99, you'll switch on the spot.

Producers supply the products these demand curves relate to, so they prefer customers have only a few (or, even better, no) substitutes for their products. Accepting that most industries have to have some level of competition, to avoid monopolies, a lack of substitutes gives producers a greater ability to make profits. If demand for your product or service is relatively inelastic, you can withstand a lot of market shocks because consumers will always prefer your goods ... unless they can't get them.

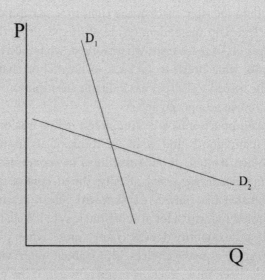

Figure 9.1:   Steeper (D_1) and flatter (D_2) demand

For companies whose products had few substitutes before the pandemic, Covid limited supplies and forced consumers to consider a wide range of new possibilities for substitutes — including going without and not buying at all. This forced test drive was a threat to *future* profitability. Once consumers know about another choice, or that they're okay not having it at all, the demand curve flattens, and the game is permanently changed.

The process of learning about substitutes is handled better in strategy than it is in economics. Economics usually says there are or there aren't substitutes. Strategy is focused on creative competitive advantage, so it helps connect a path between what is and isn't a substitute. Strategy also defines things like *isolating mechanisms* — ways to prevent competitors from copying your benefit or cost drivers. Both economics and strategy discuss *entry deterrence* or *barriers to entry*, any activity to keep competitors out of your industry. Many firms did this well pre-pandemic, but when your product simply isn't on the shelf anymore, customers being forced to try alternatives can blow these strategies out of the water. Let's see how:

A well-established brand name is in itself an entry deterrent. We all know of products that have become synonymous with their dominant brands: Kleenex (tissues), Q-tips (cotton swab), Band-Aid (adhesive bandage), iPhone (any cell phone). Sure, it's an evolution... once it becomes a verb, it loses some of its protective value. (e.g., people start "xeroxing" things on a Canon printer). Still, one point of trying to establish a dominant, well-known brand name is to deter entry.

So, let's talk toilet paper. Once upon a (semi-modern) time, the toilet paper provided in outhouses was just pages from the Sears catalogue or a repeat-use rag (ew). The first affordable, disposable toilet papers were more durable than they were gentle. Eventually, around the 1960s, we had Charmin, the squeezeably soft brand that made Mr. Whipple famous. Today's aisles are stocked full (well, usually) of brands of every kind, from soft one-ply and two-ply to renewable bamboo, flushable wet-wipes, and everything in between. In the US, where we have some of the best toilet paper on the planet (what a weird thing to brag about), people settled into their choice of brands based on attributes, prices, and prior experience. Before Covid, it was difficult to get consumers to re-evaluate their brand choice for something like toilet paper. Really, how many people thought about substitutes for toilet paper? Sure, there are moments in life when one looks down at the empty cardboard spindle, mutters something about the previous user (even if it was yourself), and grabs the nearest box of Kleenex, but those emergency substitutes were just that: emergencies. They were short-run replacements. No one ever thought to *permanently* replace toilet paper with tissues, especially since tissues are more expensive per package.

During Covid, some of us had to go days or weeks without our favorite brand of toilet paper. What did we do? We tried other brands and other options (bidet) in a forced test drive. For a certain number of people, the saving product ended up becoming the new favorite. Covid helped the substitute become an option, which then grew to be the preferred purchase over time.

Sure, this didn't happen to everybody. Now that supply chains have somewhat normalized and there are fewer limits per customer, many have returned to their old preferences. But, maybe a few people will now augment their traditional toilet paper with some of the wet wipes that they were forced to use. Maybe others don't mind buying the less expensive store brand anymore. Maybe the eco-friendly alternatives have become replacements for people who want to save the planet while they went to the bathroom. As marginal as these consumer changes are, they add up — especially for big brand holders like Procter & Gamble and Keebler.

Covid impacted the global economy, and we are continuing to see effects on labor, supply, and distribution markets today. The exact ripple effects will not be known for decades, but what we can say is that the effect of lockdowns and uncertainty was attenuated by one thing: the Internet. Had similar shutdowns happened half a century earlier — well within the lifetime of many readers — the options that "got us through," like online ordering, same-day delivery, and remote work capabilities simply wouldn't have been available. They hadn't been invented yet.

Marketing had been moving to digital platforms for many years before Covid. Losing the commuter driving to the office didn't seriously impact marketing, since radio commercials and billboards are a small part of most business' marketing effort. Cord-cutting was a bigger problem. TV viewership had started to move away from network and cable-based stations toward commercial-free (or nearly commercial-free) streaming services. This trend was accelerated by Covid lockdowns when more people were staying home. So, while there were more eyes on the TV for more hours, they weren't necessarily watching commercials. Increased exposure to the medium didn't necessarily increase exposure to the message. Add to this the impact of canceled sporting events, award shows, and other spectator gatherings that usually draw big advertising revenues, and Covid caused a major decline in advertising ROI across the board.

Market data are the most available of all business analytics, so we know more about the effect of Covid on short- and long-term profitability every day. Covid's effect on *Marketing*, however, has always been clear: by changing how we interact with one another, the pandemic changed how we receive the information on which we base our purchasing decisions.

Mini Case: Gillette

Gillette has been producing razors and other personal grooming products since 1901. The company was acquired in 2005 by Proctor & Gamble for $57 Billion. Historically, Gillette products had both high margins and a dominant market share, a perfect recipe for profits for P&G. But, despite established entry deterrents, profits always bring new competitors in eventually. And enter they did. In the mid-2010s, Harry's and Dollar Shave Club brought high-quality, lower-priced razors and other grooming products to market, starting with a free online subscription service and expanding to brick-and-mortar retailers.

Gillette's response to this was unfortunate. A brief, baseless patent infringement lawsuit in 2018 against Harry's produced only bad public relations for Gillette and provided Harry's with the one thing it needed: a lot of free public attention. Building on this bad momentum, Gillette released a controversial advertising campaign in 2019. Channeling one of its old taglines, "The best a man can get," Gillette tried to ride the social wave related to social movements by running a commercial it called "Toxic Masculinity," complete with the tagline "The best a man can be." While it was trying to make a commercial that was anti-bullying (a perfectly fine idea), the commercial was badly executed and poorly received. Since 2020, Harry's has signed a major contract with Target stores and expanded to include low-cost, high-quality women's razors. It continues to eat into Gillette's market share across multiple products, including shaving creams, balms, and hair treatments.

Gillette was truly reeling when Covid hit, the lockdowns occurred, and cash-strapped consumers couldn't afford Gillette's high-end products. Like all consumer product companies, P&G is still sifting the data to better understand how all things Covid impacted their product lines. But let's make a few guesses.

How do you think overall razor sales were impacted by Covid? What factors probably moved consumers from Gillette products to its competitors?

Harry's and Dollar Shave Club offered free trials to new customers. They started delivering samples by mail, since that was their original distribution method. What's the idea behind that?

Along the way, Gillette tried to respond with its own free trial. Since it had a dominant market share, was that the best response?

Gillette ran a Super Bowl ad in 2022, the first one they've had in over a decade. Research that ad and see if you can find anything interesting (perhaps ironic) about it.

Discussion Questions

9.1 Advertising is expensive. Television commercials and video pop-up ads cost a lot of money and need to have a bit of a shelf life. So, businesses have to make decisions about their near-term future before they make those advertising expenditures. Will their market still be "masked," contactless, off-site, and so on? The "evergreen" solution is to market the product that will probably be around forever. Starbucks and Applebee's Casual Dining restaurant are running ads that show happy mask-less families bouncing back into their stores and being joyously greeted by mask-less employees. What are the pros and cons of this advertising strategy?

9.2 Test driving in the form of free samples is a popular way to introduce new products. Costco was a frequent participant in this approach, as were several grocery chains. Samples went away during lockdown and are back now with new limitations, like additional wrapping on the samples. Those new requirements will change what things can be sampled. Describe why this matters.

9.3 Marketing and advertising during a pandemic aren't strategies people learn about in school. Messaging needs to be realistic, but at the same time optimistic. Many companies chose to connect products and brands with support and sponsorship of healthcare workers and first responders. That's similar to the traditional approach (during normal times) of using spokespeople who are famous athletes or movie stars. Interestingly, Covid commercials might be just as effective while being less expensive. Explain.

9.4 As time passed and we became a little more accepting of Covid and how it was changing our world, marketing professionals had to consider a new trade-off: lighthearted messaging versus a more somber approach. Put another way, they had to gauge in advance how receptive audiences would be to levity. Discuss the pros and cons of a funny marketing campaign as we enter the endemic phase.

9.5 The transition of marketing dollars from traditional media to digital media and social network platforms/data mining has been going on for more than a decade, but television is still the biggest outlet based on dollar expenditures. Do you think Covid and the lockdowns sped up or slowed down the transition away from television to social media?

Epilogue
Hello From the Other Side

"The only thing we know about the future is that it will be different."
— *Peter Drucker*

We've all learned a lot during our time at Covid University. We've learned how adaptable our modern world is and how vulnerable our optimized, multi-national supply chains were. We've tried new products, watched new shows (I'll join the throng recommending Apple TV's *Ted Lasso*), and we have seen far too many friends and loved ones in two dimensions.

One thing that has changed, even in the time it has taken to write this book, is what the endgame is. What does the "other side" of Covid look like? It does not look like it's a world in which we've beaten Covid and banished it to the book of things we can forget. New and more contagious variants are popping up and are likely to continue for some time. By its very nature, a pandemic turns *endemic* and part of daily life.

The other side is not going to be a return to what once was. We have turned a page and we are now going to have to move forward knowing that SARS-Cov-2, nicknamed COVID-19 by the World Health Organization to indicate it is the strain of the SARS Coronavirus that appeared in 2019, has spread around the world and will be mutating and reappearing forever. The SARS (Severe Acute Respiratory Syndrome) viruses first appeared in 2003, but spread was limited until COVID-19. So, this was, as they say, a game changer.

This game has been played many times before in human history. The Black Plague killed tens of millions — perhaps as many as two hundred million people. Some estimate it killed a quarter of the population of the planet. But, once its cause was discovered and modern medicine kicked in, it was found to be completely curable and largely preventable. Viral pandemics like the 1918 Spanish Flu, the 1957 Asian Flu, and COVID-19 are much trickier foes. Immunizations help and there are symptomatic treatments, but viruses mutate quickly (as we all have learned). The response to the early strains of Covid were economically draconian: lockdowns, online schooling, restaurant and bar closures, etc. But then there was hope: with incredible speed, the scientific community developed vaccines and hundreds of millions of people protected themselves and their communities. Not wishing to remind everyone of the past two years, let's just say we humans got a little cocky. Honestly, they will run out of Greek letters before this is done. No one knows, of course, but even the short duration of the Covid timeline was enough to significantly change certain aspects of human behavior. That's why we believe many of the changes we've seen in the economy are here to stay.

Here's the problem: making long-run economic predictions in print, in a book, is always risky, let along while we're still analyzing the business and economic lessons of COVID-19. This book has shown the myriad variables one must consider when making predictions. There isn't one way of looking at the data, and there isn't one easy solution for every problem, so we're going to avoid too many specifics. We won't predict the long-run success or failure of any particular company. Instead, we'll focus on factors that were already underway that Covid exacerbated or accelerated.

These factors include trends like online shopping, which was already hurting bricks and mortar retail. They also include the proliferation of streaming services and affordable high-definition televisions, which were already hurting attendance at movie theaters. We have talked about firms that were already experimenting flexible working environments and remote capabilities prior to Covid. These trends all play into the factors that define the *macroeconomy*.

Concept Review: Macroeconomics

There are very important aspects of "the other side" that can be gleaned from macroeconomics. Most business students and businesspeople have had a class or some other interaction with this area of study. The economics we've discussed so far, microeconomics, deals with individual markets, supply and demand, and personal choices that govern what individual firms and consumers do. Macroeconomics, on the other hand, looks at the whole economy.

Using the basic market model — supply and demand — as the template, macroeconomics looks at the output of the entire economy (called Real Gross Domestic Product or *Real GDP*) and the price of all goods (called the *GDP Deflator*). Because there are a lot of factors, macroeconomists use aggregated proxies to measure progress. These proxies typically align with GDP. For example, everything in the economy is produced by people working, so they calculate an unemployment rate. That's statistic comes from a monthly survey. There are also measures of prices that are easier to calculate than a full list of prices (but somewhat less accurate), like the *Consumer Price Index* (*CPI*). These factors can be used in economies all over the world, from individual nations to larger trading partnerships, like *NAFTA*.

What we're trying to do in macroeconomics is determine if the economy is doing the best it can, in some overall sense. We usually use recent history to create a benchmark, so we ask things like:

How does current Real GDP compare with recent history?
How does the current unemployment rate compare to recent history?
How do overall prices or *inflation*, the rate of change in all prices, compare with recent history?

Various models have emerged to study the macroeconomy, and there are entire books on each one. Some use these major indicators, and some don't. Because the effects of COVID-19 were on people, we will use them. Let's talk about Covid's effects on unemployment, real GDP, and inflation.

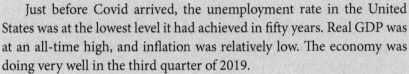

Just before Covid arrived, the unemployment rate in the United States was at the lowest level it had achieved in fifty years. Real GDP was at an all-time high, and inflation was relatively low. The economy was doing very well in the third quarter of 2019.

Then came Covid. Fearing a calamitous epidemic and heeding mounting evidence, local, state, and federal governments closed a big chunk of their economies. This, of course, caused Real GDP to plummet and unemployment to skyrocket across the board. Here in the US, many people described this as a *recession* or a *depression*, the terms used for earlier downturns in the economy, but this event was different. It wasn't caused by free-operating economic forces; Covid shocks and mandated protections caused a significant decrease in production and consumption in industries across the world.

Why does it matter why it happened? Because the cure for any economic shock is dependent on what caused it. Early in Lockdown, as people began talking about an endgame (prematurely), there were those who correctly identified that the cure for the current downturn was to end lockdowns and re-open consumption and production. To do this, we needed to control Covid, so vaccines and treatments became the main focus of investment and regulation.

Jump ahead to the first quarter of 2022. Real GDP has completely recovered, and unemployment is back close to its pre-Covid, historical low. The main issue we continue to have, in a macroeconomic sense, is inflation. Overall prices are rising at the highest rate than we've seen in decades. But the macroeconomic problem — the decline in Real GDP and the increase in unemployment — has been resolved. Things are back to where they were pre-Covid … right?

Let's go back to our discussion of data, way back in the beginning of this book. Macroeconomics aggregates data — it gathers everything together and assumes away a lot of nuances to arrive at a single indicator of economic health. Real GDP is the sum of everything we produce (goods and services) times a fixed set of prices (to eliminate the effect of inflation). In saying Real GDP is "back to where it was", we are ignoring the fact that this is a completely different economy. Thousands of businesses closed. While the unemployment rate has declined, this is in part due to many people — about three million as of January 2022 — no longer working and no longer seeking jobs. How can Real GDP be back to where we started?

The answer is: we are doing different things. Covid itself has created new jobs. Thousands of healthcare professionals are being paid to administer vaccines and Covid tests. Thousands of people are being paid to join legions of home-delivery professionals, as people continue to value home delivery in lieu of store and restaurant visits. This is not the same Real GDP as before Covid, it's just the same overall size. Arguably, it's also not as good. One thing we are aware of in macroeconomics is that "bads" are still goods. Not all jobs are things we want; but they all count toward GDP.

It will take a while before the dust settles, macroeconomically speaking. We (hopefully) won't have the direct Covid-related spending forever; surely we won't all need three shots in a year, every year. But, the economy will have lost some jobs, some goods, and some components of GDP permanently, and we don't know what will come to replace those things.

There are micro (individual market and business level changes) and macro (economy-wide differences) issues in the economy drawing from our Covid experience. This pandemic has dramatically accelerated the economy's move to online shopping, online at-home entertainment, and other internet-based aspects of the economy. To some extent, consumers have found that there are options where the final good is exactly the same (online shopping with same-day service is pretty much the same as going to the store) or similar (streaming movies with big screen TVs) than before the pandemic. Some producers have found cost advantages too, and Covid pushed them further down an existing/better path.

The movie theater industry was moving toward convenience and increased services before Covid and facing a much bigger threat from at-home alternatives. Those changes will almost certainly be accelerated. Comfortable recliner chairs, reserved seating, and meal service were all part of the pre-Covid movie theater makeover. Convincing people to get dressed, drive and park their car, leave their at-home recliner, their

kitchen, their cleaner bathroom, and the ability to pause the movie they are watching on the 80-inch OLED TV might be a much bigger proposition.

Movie distributors always controlled the fate of movie theaters by deciding where movies would be released. With so many movies being produced by and specifically for streaming services like Netflix, Amazon Prime, and Disney Plus, the exclusive access to content those theaters once had is now also disappearing. Putting all of this together, it's a virtual certainty that the movie theater industry will never return to its formal glory.

Like movie theaters, bricks-and-mortar retail was struggling before lockdowns, masks, and other Covid responses and it's almost certain that we'll see the demise of several iconic retailers. Years ago, many of us predicted a morphed version of clothing and related retailers which was a small footprint, "try on store" that had inventory only for the purposes of test drives. It was hypothesized that it would be supported by a home delivery infrastructure that provided low-price final goods. Retail innovation might not go that way. Trying on clothes using the camera on your smartphone is already here and the technology will only get better. The necessity driving these innovations — the high cost of inventory, rent, and personnel related to retail operations — has only grown during Covid. This means that the threats to major department stores that existed pre-Covid were accelerated, and are even greater today.

A good way to think about how Covid is affecting retail is similar to the last adopters in the smartphone story that we discussed earlier. Grandma and Grandpa finally got rid of their flip phone (or land line) during Lockdown because they needed Facetime to stay in touch with the grandchildren. Similarly, the people who had not been active online shoppers pre-Covid almost certainly started shopping online. Amazon and other online retailers are easy to use and reliable. They have enormous advantages, like 24 hr. access and no crowded parking lots to navigate. They were winning before Covid. In sports parlance, now, it's a runaway.

The restaurant industry will also change, but this one is harder to predict. Home-delivered meal services (DoorDash, Grub Hub, Uber Eats, and others) grew dramatically during the Covid experience, by some accounts as much as 300%, but none of these companies are currently profitable. They could end up like Peloton and other companies that sniffed success during Covid but still don't have a strategy for long-term success. They could be lucky. On the other hand, they might find themselves targets for consolidation and become integrated into a larger industry-wide strategy. Time will tell.

One thing is certain: the increase in volume of food-delivery services, what restaurant industry insiders call the "take-out boom," has every indication of being around in the long run. Like going to a department store at the mall, going out to eat has lots of transaction costs. Getting reasonably dressed, drive time, parking, wait time (which can be used for other things at home), etc. are all added to the price of the meal. As restaurants learn how to adjust menus and package food better, the at-home version of the restaurant meal will continue to be more popular.

Californians have long-admired the hamburger chain In-n-Out, but its business model is one that might grow post-Covid. Very few restaurants in this chain have indoor, sit-down tables available. Its menu is very small compared to its peers, so its cost structure is limited, and inventory is easier to manage. The chain provides affordable, high-quality burgers and fries that most customers have taken home to eat since the 1950s. One can imagine restaurants that combine the home-delivered model of Domino's and other pizza companies and the fast, efficient drive-up model of In-n-Out into a single, small-footprint outlet.

A lot more work-from-home is also here to stay, but the nature of work, the specific requirements of the job, will change. Companies will need to find ways to recreate synergies and establish more subtle forms of communication while meeting demand. Every job has some combination of basic tasks and more complex, interactive skills that are unique to its industry. Pre-Covid, we saw many basic tasks being outsourced, offshored, or automated. The Covid experience, including the Great Resignation, has given employers a way to re-evaluate their make vs. buy decisions. They have a better sense of which jobs have to be done in-house and which ones can be outsourced or replaced with a robot software package.

Macroeconomically and socially, people are learning a lot about what matters to them. Human interactions like sports, sporting events, clubs, churches, and many others are making a big comeback. Covid taught us that people need people. Businesses are reckoning with the fact that they, too, are composed of people, and they can no longer ignore the priorities of the human beings that support them. In this way, the positive effects of Covid will continue to push the evolution toward the better business practices of the future. We can only hope this future is one where people are valued, companies are agile, and everyone is prepared.

Mini Case: The Future of the Grocery Store

Pre-Covid, Kroger was the second largest grocery chain in the US. Kroger stores are traditional grocery stores, in that its stores sell fresh and perishable products like meat and produce, longer-term perishables like bread products, refrigerated products like dairy, a variety of frozen foods, and several aisles of non-perishable canned goods. In most cases, they also sell prepared foods and a delicatessen with meats and cheeses sliced to order.

Covid showed that people do not particularly want or need to spend hours shopping for groceries. Many people happily delegated the shopping experience to a store employee who then carried the order to the car waiting in the parking lot. Suppose that mentality takes hold. Let's think about the products we've described and consider new ways to shop for groceries.

Arguably, about half of the food in a grocery store can be purchased online and delivered with no risk to quality or flavor. Nonperishable goods run the gamut from canned soup to coffee to potato chips to soda. Based on inventory cost savings online retailers have experienced in their grocery delivery test drives, these goods could also be made available at a lower price to consumers. Since online retailer Amazon already owns a grocery store (Whole Foods) and traditional grocery stores Target and Walmart both have well-functioning online applications, it's hard to imagine a future where groceries won't have a significant, expansive online component. Indeed, in 2020, Kroger position as the second-largest grocery in the country was usurped. The new #2, with only 36 storefronts nationwide: Amazon.com.

New grocery competitors like Aldi and Trader Joes are already operating much smaller stores with much less variety in the nonperishable aisles. Even Costco and other warehouse stores that offer larger quantities of most goods that they sell have only one or two options, less than a typical grocery store.

In addition, several innovations in food packaging have allowed some perishables to last much longer. Packaging fresh meat in air-tight containers that have carbon dioxide, nitrogen, or oxygen increase the shelf life of fresh meat by a week or more. New forms of pasteurization have dramatically increased the shelf life of dairy products as well. Arguably, dairy products are easier to imagine moving out of the traditional store and into an online shopping format. Similarly, frozen food and bread products can easily become online grocery items if packed well.

Prepared foods, sometimes called grab-and-go, are not a particularly profitable part of most stores. In most cases, these goods have a very short shelf life (often a day), and many stores lose money on this segment. The $5 rotisserie chicken at Costco is a famous *loss leader*. So, we'll let the restaurant industry and its new focus on takeout food have that part of the grocery store back. That leaves meats and produce, and they're trickier. Many people strongly prefer selecting their own meats and veggies. If that's it, the innovative solution might be fun.

Let's ponder what the future of the grocery industry looks like. If grocery stores become (primarily) meats and produce, but stores do still exist, can you describe a hybrid delivery model where the rest of your order is not delivered to your home?

Discussion Questions

10.1 In thinking about the future of restaurants, consider the business model we call the "all you can eat buffet." Given the things people liked (variety, quantity) about that style of restaurant, do you think they will come back?

10.2 Health-based information technology was a wave of the future even before Covid. Smart watches were getting better at monitoring certain vital signs, and it is possible that smartphones could use cameras and other sensory functions to do more health screening (glucose monitoring is already possible). Virtual doctors' appointments became a reality during the Covid era. Discuss the limits of this future use of home technology.

10.3 It appears as if the endemic phase of the Covid timeline will have a lot more work-from-home employment opportunities — but not every job can be done at home. Still, this is one explanation of the Great Resignation. Why?

10.4 Disney owns some of the most lucrative movie franchises in the world: Star Wars, the Marvel Universe, Pixar, and of course, Disney's original classics. Disney, to some extent, will control the future of the movie theater business. If it decides to release all future films on Disney+ (perhaps at the same time that it is released in the theater, and perhaps for an additional fee), how will that affect box office and movie theater revenues?

10.5 What will be the biggest difference in your life when we finally do get to the other side of our Covid experience?

Glossary of Companies & Brands

Alphabet: the corporate owner of Google, YouTube, and several other digital businesses. They have become one of the world's foremost data analytics platforms. Website: https://abc.xyz.

Amazon: a Washington-state based US firm that has a large, online retail business, several digital streaming services, and one of the largest internet backbone platforms: Amazon Web Services, known as AWS. Website: https://amazon.com.

AMC: the largest chain of movie theaters in the world. Website: https://amc.com.

Apple: a California firm that designs and sell smartphones, tablets, laptops, smart watches, and related peripherals. It also has music, video, and other steaming services. It is the most valuable firm, based on market value, in the world as of this writing. Website: https://apple.com.

Aquafina: a brand of bottled water produced by PepsiCo. Website: https://pepsico.com.

Baskin Robbins: a US-based multinational ice cream and related products restaurant chain. Website: https://baskinrobbins.com.

Blockbuster: a now defunct video rental and retail chain. The company's streaming service is now owned and operated by Dish Network. Website: https://blockbuster.com.

Blue Apron: a meal kit company that delivers portioned and prepared meal ingredients ready to be cooked. Website: https://blueparon.com.

Campbells Soup: a well-known US-based canned soup brand. Website: https://campbells.com.

Carvana: a used car company that buys and sells cars using an online platform and a pick-up and delivery approach. Website: https://carvana.com.

Charmin: a popular brand of toilet paper produced by US consumer products company Proctor and Gamble. Website: https://us.pg.com.

Cheesecake Factory: a casual dining restaurant chain that features a variety of cheesecakes among its dessert options. Website: https://thecheesecakefactory.com.

Chef Boyardee: a popular US-based brand of canned spaghetti and other Italian cuisine. It is produced and sold by US-based Conagra Brands. Website: https://conagra.com.

Chick-fil-A: a US fast food company that specializes in chicken-based products. Website: https://chick-fil-a.com.

Clorox: a US-based brand of cleaners, primarily bleach. Website: https://Clorox.com.

Coach: a US-based designer of handbags, luggage, and other leather goods. It is owned by Tapestry, Inc. Website: https://tapestry.com.

Costco: the dominant, membership-based, warehouse-style retailer in the US. Website: https://costco.com.

Dasani: a brand of bottled water produced by Coca-Cola. Website: https://us.coca-cola.com.

Del Monte: a US brand of canned fruits and vegetables. Website: https://delmonte.com.

Disney: a US-based entertainment conglomerate that operates theme parks, television networks, Disney+ streaming service, and several movie production companies. Their movie and related catalogue includes Pixar,

Lucasfilms (Star Wars), Marvel Comics (Superheroes), and Disney's classic animated characters. Website: https://disney.com.

Dollar Shave Club: a US company that sells shaving products. They were originally a membership-based retailer, but their razors and other products are now sold at many major retailers. Website: https://dollarshaveclub.com.

Domino's: a US-based multinational pizza and related foods restaurant chain. Website: https://dominos.com.

DoorDash: a restaurant food delivery service. Website: https://doordash.com.

Facebook: the world's largest social media platform. Website: https://facebook.com.

Ferragamo's: an Italian designer of luxury shoes and accessories. Website: https://ferragamo.com.

Gillette: the largest shaving and related grooming products company in the US. It is owned by US-based consumer products company Proctor and Gamble. Website: https://us.pg.com.

Gojo: the US-based manufacturer of Purell brand hand sanitizer. Website: https://gojo.com.

Google: the largest search engine (by far!) in the world. It is owned by Alphabet. Website: https://google.com.

Grubhub: a restaurant food delivery service. Website: https://grubhub.com.

Gucci: an Italian-based designer of luxury shoes, handbags, and other fashion accessories. Website: https://www.gucci.com.

Harry's Razor: a US-based company that sells razors and other related shaving and grooming products. Website: https://harrys.com.

In-n-Out: a popular, primarily California-based hamburger chain. Most of its restaurants are drive-through or walk-up only; they have no inside seating. Website: https://www.in-and-out.com.

Jimmy Choo's: a UK-based retailer that specializes in luxury shoes, handbags, and other accessories. Website: https://www.us.jimmychoo.com.

Johnson & Johnson: a US-based conglomerate known for many famous consumer-based healthcare products (Band-Aids bandages for example). Their Janssen Pharmaceuticals subsidiary developed a vaccine that was effective against COVID-19. Website: https://www.jnj.com.

KFC: the largest fried chicken-oriented restaurant chain in the world and the second largest restaurant chain (McDonalds is the largest). Website: https://www.kfc.com.

K-Mart: a now defunct big box department store. It was once the largest department store chain in the world. Website: https://www.kmart.com.

Lamborghini: an Italian designer and manufacturer of luxury sports cars. Website: https://www.lamborghini.com.

McDonald's: a pioneering fast-food restaurant chain, originally specializing in hamburgers but now featuring a large, diverse menu. It is the largest restaurant chain in the world. Website: https://www.mcdonalds.com.

Meta: the new corporate name for Facebook. Website: https://www.about.facebook.com/meta.

Microsoft: the Washington State-based software company and one of the largest companies in the world by market value. Their video conferencing software Microsoft Teams became very popular during the Covid lockdowns. Website: https://www.microsoft.com.

Moderna: a research and development focused biotechnology company that specializes in messenger RNA, known as mRNA therapies. They were one of the companies that found an effective vaccine against COVID-19. Website: https://www.modernatx.com.

Netflix: a US-based company that primarily operates the world's biggest streaming service. Website: https://www.netflix.com.

NordicTrack: an exercise equipment company founded in 1975 that makes treadmills, stationary bicycles, and the like. Website: https://www.nordictrack.com.

Orangetheory: a US fitness and exercise studio franchise-based business that became popular in the decade before Covid. https://www.orangetheory. com.

Peloton: an exercise equipment company whose equipment is integrated with a video screen that, for an additional fee, will connect the user to a trainer or a class. Website: https://www.onepeloton.com.

Pfizer: a US-based pharmaceutical company. Partnering with the German company BioNTech, Pfizer was one of the companies that came up with a vaccine that was effective against Covid. Website: https://www.pfizer.com.

Planet Fitness: a US operator and franchisor of exercise and fitness centers. Website: https://www.planetfitness.com.

Postmates: a restaurant and grocery food delivery service. Website: https:// www.postmates.com.

Procter & Gamble: a large consumer products conglomerate whose well-known brands include Gillette shaving products, Crest dental products, Tide laundry products, Pampers baby products, and many others. Website: https://www.us.pg.com.

Purell: a popular brand of hand sanitizer produced by US-based Gojo. Website: https://www.gojo.com.

Q-tips: a popular brand of cotton swabs manufactured by UK-based consumer products company Unilever. Website: https://www.unilever.com.

Rolex: a Swiss-based designer and manufacturer of luxury watches. Website: https://www.rolex.com.

Shipt: US delivery service owned by retailer Target. Website: https://www. shipt.com.

Starbucks: the largest coffeehouse chain in the world. Website: https:// www.starbucks.com.

Target: a large, US-based big box department store chain. Website: https:// www.target.com.

Tesla: a US-based designer and manufacturer of electric cars, batteries, and related technologies. Website: https://www.tesla.com.

Uber Eats: a restaurant food delivery service that was launched by the ridesharing service company Uber. Website: https://www.ubereats.com.

Ulta: a US-based cosmetics and beauty products retailer. Website: https://www.ulta.com.

Walmart: the largest retailer in the world. Website: https://www.walmart.com.

WebEx: video conferencing software platform owned by US-based Cisco. Website: https://www.cisco.com.

Zoom: formally known as Zoom Video Communications, a US-based software developer whose video conferencing software became popular during Covid. Website: https://zoom.us.

Glossary of Terms

Agency Cost: deriving from what's called the Principal–Agent problem in economics, the cost associated with monitoring and incentivizing those to whom tasks have been delegated.

Average Cost: total cost divided by total current output.

Benefit Drivers: in strategy, the consumer or demand-side factors that allow some firms to remain profitable even after entry has occurred.

Bureaucracy Cost: the operational cost associated with an organizations structure or bureaucracy.

Competitive Advantage: in strategy, the company or product level factors that allow a company to make and maintain profits even after entry has occurred.

Complements: goods that are used at the same time or in concert with one another.

Conglomerate: a company that owns a large and diverse collection of other companies.

Coordination Costs: the operational cost associated with aligning the timing of input acquisition with input usage.

Corporate Culture: the operational rules, norms, standards, and processes that companies use to structure the human side of their company.

Cost Drivers: in strategy, the producer or supply-side factors that allow some firms to remain profitable even after entry has occurred.

Demand: in economics, the relationship between price and quantity from the consumer's perspective. For most goods, most of the time, this is an inverse relationship; as price rises, the quantity demanded falls.

Diminishing Marginal Utility: the assertion that happiness rises at a decreasing rate as we consume more of any one good at any one time.

Directive Leadership: a mode of leadership that involves giving directions or orders.

Diseconomies of scale: the increase in average cost the many companies experience as output rises beyond minimum average cost. This is usually due to increasing variable costs as the firm reaches capacity.

Economies of scale: the decline in average cost that most businesses experience as they increase output. This is usually due to sharing fixed costs across more units.

Elastic: see elasticity.

Elasticity: a way to measure the steepness of the demand or supply curve that avoids (among other things) the problem that units cause when one uses slopes. Rather than change in price divided by change in quantity, which could look big or small depending on units used, elasticity uses percentage change in price and percentage change in quantity, which is unit free. (And, unlike slope, elasticity has the percentage change in quantity on top.) A "steep" demand is said to be inelastic, which means the percentage in quantity is smaller than the percentage in price. A "flat" demand is said to be elastic; the percentage in quantity is bigger than the percentage in price.

Empowering Leadership: a mode of leadership in which the leader (sometimes called a super-leader) motivated the followers to self-manage or self-lead.

Fixed Costs: the part of the cost of producing a good that doesn't change as you increase your output in the short run. Fixed costs are usually things that we think of as "land and capital" including things like factories, machinery, and the like.

GDP: Gross Domestic Product, the most commonly used measure for what's called national output. It is the value of all final goods and services produced by the citizens of a country during a year (or some other period of time.)

Inelastic: see elasticity.

Jollies: a made-up unit of happiness used in the exposition of utility theory.

Make vs. Buy: the decision on the part of the firm as to whether they will make or buy their inputs.

Marginal Cost: the change in total cost as you change your output. Marginal cost, in economics, is the short-run supply curve.

Macroeconomics: the area of economics that focuses on the overall state of the entire economy. Issues such as unemployment and inflation are often discussed.

Microeconomics: the area of economics that focuses on individual consumers and individual producers. It includes what's called consumer theory and theory of the firm; the theories try to explain the observed behavior of consumers and producers.

Privacy: in strategy, the make vs. buy factor that is concerned with protecting important product attributes, secret formulae, trade secrets, and the like.

Qualitative Data: data that are based on the qualities of important attributes that are observed by the researcher.

Quantitative Data: data that take the form of numbers.

Substitutes: goods that are used in lieu of one another.

Supply: in economics, the relationship between price and quantity from the producer's perspective. For most goods, most of the time, this is a positive relationship; as price rises, the quantity supplied also rises.

Test Drive: sampling, using, or in general trying a product before you buy it.

Total Cost: in economics, the sum of fixed and variable costs.

Transactional Leadership: a mode of leadership in which the leader motivates the follower with various forms of compensation or punishment.

These include not only things like money but also praise, promotion, scolding, and demotion.

Transactions Costs: in economics, any cost associated with making a transaction. These could include search cost, opportunity cost, contracting costs, and the costs associated with potential litigation.

Transformational Leadership: a mode of leadership that involves inspiring followers to grow, create, innovate, and transform.

Tribal Culture: the organizational rules, norms, standards, and processes that groups of people use to organize their societies.

Utility: happiness.

Utility Theory: based on the observation that people don't consume large amounts of any one good at any one time, it is the model that posits that happiness (utility) rises at a decreasing rate as we consume any one good at any one time.

Variable Costs: the part of the cost of producing a good that does change as you increase your output in the short run. Variable costs are usually things like labor, raw materials, and utilities (electricity).

Notes on Discussion Questions

1.1 This question is very much a set of discussion questions intended to engage students in the exercise of looking at Covid from a personal and business perspective.

1.2 It needs to get more formal but not necessarily less personal. We can analyze both quantitative and qualitative data. But a lot of what we know now is very much self-reported stories or what might be called oral histories.

1.3 This particular earthquake brought down or damaged virtually every unreinforced masonry building in the city, which led to a major change in building codes and their enforcement across the US.

1.4 Both of these financial crashes led to increase in regulation of financial markets. The 1929 crash led to limits in margin trading (and ultimately to the creation of the Securities and Exchange Commission) and the 2008 crisis brought forth new regulations of financial derivatives and the entire banking industry.

1.5 This is mostly a discussion question but 9/11 comes to mind and the subsequent changes in airport and cockpit security.

2.1 Most assuredly not. Like the fans in the stands, people learned how important the shared experience of eating and drinking with others was. These are important lessons for customers and businesses alike. Jollies come from many different aspects of a consumption good.

2.2 The importance of networking; the importance of interpersonal connections; the importance of knowledge sharing; the importance of learning first-hand about new products, new approaches, innovations. The list goes on. And these things will take quite a long time to figure out. The short-run cost savings is easy to see. The long-run benefits lost will be harder to assess.

2.3 Popular brands bank on people not wanting to risk a bad experience by trying something new. But there's a price; quite literally, the high price of most major brand-name products. Discovering, perhaps under duress, because your favorite brand wasn't available, that there was a cheaper alternative that was "just as good" was great for you, not so much for the brand-name company. Example???

2.4 The problem with the value proposition is that the customer for education is not who (what) you think. Convenience, predictability, etc. all favor online schooling, but that assumes the customer is exclusively the student. Narrowing the problem down a bit, consider online MBA programs. The point of an MBA is to get students the skills that allow them to get a job in the business world. So, the customer is students AND employers. Online is convenient; does it teach the skills that employers want as well?

2.5 Salespeople. New and used car salespeople and the bureaucracy (I'll have to talk to my manager about your offer…) have proven to be unnecessary if the Carvana model is correct.

2.6 Like many Covid experiences, the no-touch doctor's visit was already here. A check-up had become a check of your vitals (temperature, blood pressure, etc.), probably some blood tests, and a doctor (maybe!) asking a bunch of questions and putting your answer into a computer or I-pad. With the availability of do-it-yourself home testing equipment, you don't really need to go the doctor's office anymore for a check-up. But as the question says, there are things that cannot be done this way. There's no such thing as a virtual dental visit or a virtual tooth scraping for that matter. The line in the sand between office visit and virtual is, like many things, a matter of which of the five senses you need to use for the health issue involved.

3.1 New product launches. As we'll discuss later, Disney launched its streaming service at the very beginning of the Covid crisis. Since everyone was learning about streaming and steaming services, they got a boost from lockdowns.

3.2 Not likely; at least not many. But it probably does mean that jobs will be moving around a bit. Between Covid and other disruptions, the cost of a far-flung supply chain has been highlighted for most companies. The key to understanding an optimized, low-cost supply chain is correctly incorporating all costs. If your "low cost" input is stuck in transit in the middle of a large body of water (like the Pacific Ocean), it really isn't as low cost as you thought. The upshot is lower labor costs will have to be balanced with other higher costs. The likely beneficiaries, as far as jobs are concerned, for US-based companies will be countries in Central and South America.

3.3 The key to this discussion is understanding what various skilled professional people do, how necessary it is, and how "replaceable" it is. Can the job of a firefighter in Los Angeles be outsourced to Taiwan? Can it be done by a robot? What about an accountant in Los Angeles? Can that person's work be done by someone in India or by a computer?

3.4 Fried chicken. With all due respect to Colonial Sanders and KFC's special way of making fried chicken, Grocery stores and in some places even convenience stores (Royal Farms, a 200-store chain of convenience stores on the East Coast of the US is an excellent example) can deep fry chicken pretty well.

3.5 Professors can still do a lot of one-on-one with students. Individual Zoom meetings are arguably easier because no one has to go to the office. Inspiring, classroom lectures are much harder to replicate.

4.1 Companies have been trying various ways to do this for many years. Company retreats and hiring consultants (bringing in outside "eyes") are both examples. Google "Appreciative Inquiry" for an interesting formal approach to this.

4.2 This is a classroom discussion, but look for things like inclusiveness and respect across all skill sets.

4.3 This is a classroom discussion. Try to get students to stop thinking like the employees and start think like the employers. For example, you have to find the right balance between appreciation and getting the job done. Work is work, not play.

4.4 One well-known driver of turnover is boredom. Jobs can easily revert to drudgery if they don't involve any real skill or effort. Also, feeling detached from the output or the firm's goals is a problem. Once upon a time, a skilled worker could step back at the end of a long, hard work experience and see the bridge or building or car that they had a hand in building. That created a sense of accomplishment and pride. Is that still there for most workers and most jobs?

4.5 There's a strong tendency for partners and executives in these kinds of professional firms to value the core skills (law, architecture, engineering, etc.) much more than all other skills and other employees, even equally well-educated employees. This is a good time to think about basketball. You might be the tallest player on the team. You're so tall you can just drop the ball in the hoop and score. So, your team will always win, right? Not unless your teammates pass you the ball!

5.1 This is an interesting problem. There is no obvious online substitute for non-verbal communication. One answer would be more one-on-one meetings (online) with a more personal touch. But the downside is that takes a LOT of time.

5.2 Interestingly, many of the problems with remote work pre-Covid had to do with people being in other parts of the world. Different languages, different cultures, but also different time zones. If half of your company is in California and the other half is in Singapore, someone is always in the virtual meeting at 2 am. Having the entire organization interacting online probably helped everyone get a better understanding of how well that approach could work when a lot of those other difficulties (language, time zones, etc.) were not there.

5.3 This differs from firm to firm and even industry to industry, but considering the Great Resignation the answer would appear to be its not very effective.

5.4 Probably. You'll still need the carrots and sticks of transactional leadership, but you can't wait for people to figure out how to work at home on their own. You need to instill a new mentality in people and that's empowering leadership. There's another problem, however. Those you are leading, who are called the followers, have to be "motivatable" by things other than the transactional motivators. Put differently (and with fewer made-up words), your employees have to have an innate desire to do a good job on their own. And frankly, that might not be the same employees that you had pre-Covid.

5.5 This is a discussion question. Many things were tried during Covid from virtual holiday parties to virtual happy hours. Discuss which, if any of those sorts of things, felt like they worked.

5.6 Think about things that cannot be done at home: new designs, market changing innovations, things that involve using the company's "secret formula." The risk of catching Covid or anything else has to be balanced with the risk of losing the things that make your company profitable.

6.1 Unfortunately for Blue Apron and similar companies, this list of potential competitors is long: Any grocery store, Amazon (which owns a grocery store but has other advantages), Walmart and Target, and even some restaurant chains.

6.2 Existing competitors include Microsoft (Teams), Cisco (AnyConnect), Google Meet, Go-To-Meeting, and many others. Zoom had some advantages that were short lived: it was relatively easy to use, and it had a cute, catchy name. But those benefit drivers didn't create long-term profits.

6.3 No. Bidets weren't new. And they aren't a perfect substitute for toilet paper.

6.4 People had much more time on their hands during the lockdowns, they literally ran out of things to do. Almost everyone has a book or two that they intended to read when they had the time. So a lot of people did just that. It's doubtful that this will represent a long-term increase in the number of books that people read post-Covid.

6.5 Between the economic uncertainties and the inability to see doctors or easily access hospitals, the opportunity cost of having a baby was much higher during the worst part of the Covid experience.

7.1 Skipping mistakes. Learning from the first mover's mistakes. Not having to build the demand for the new product. Not having to get rules or regulations changed.

7.2 Co-branding is a good way to increase sales of both goods. People who need their Starbucks fix will probably order some stuff from Target while they are there. And people needing to pick-up some pampers from target might realize they need a double shot espresso.

7.3 Reliability became far more important than it ever was when a huge chunk of the economy was virtual. Customer service was never the cornerstone of cable companies and other internet service providers. Going forward, they can't be cavalier about that. Unreliable ISPs will be abandoned for ones that work with more certainty.

7.4 Apple was ordered to change how it charged app developers who used its app store in 2021. Apple has a very tightly integrated ecosystem and some people believe this is unfair.

Amazon has a diverse set of businesses, some of which — like Amazon Web Services — give it control over many other internet businesses. Some legislators in the US believe Amazon should be broken up into separate businesses like Amazon Retail, Amazon Hardware (Alexa), Amazon Streaming, and AWS.

7.5 Hand sanitizer stations were installed in many more locations around the US. Assuming they are kept and refilled, this would be a permanent increase in the hand sanitizer market.

8.1 Companies could have things one might call "work windows." Suppose you're supposed to work eight hours a day, sometimes on your own, sometimes with others but online or on the phone. Rather than leave the timing up to you or the company, suppose all of your work has to happen between 7 am and 7 pm or some other window outside of which you are not ever expected to be available by or for your work.

8.2 Disable communications and connections outside of the window. That seems unlikely, but it would be a good way to make the commitment credible.

8.3 Aside from the lost synergies, collaborations, and effortless communication, things don't always work right. When things go awry, its better to be in the office where people can legitimately see that you are working hard and doing your best. As for the firm, people working from home probably get an over-blown sense of their own ability. There are things that the firm brings to the table that people often take for granted. One example is getting the client or the customer for your product or service.

8.4 If the employer doesn't create and strictly enforce the rules, some employees would inevitably offer to work anytime so as to curry favor with their company. Knowing that, other employees might feel compelled to do the same, thus destroying the employee-driven rule.

8.5 There's a part of human nature that wants to heal, that wants to help solve problems, and that wants to alleviate suffering. But the level of work, the bureaucracy, and the realities of seeing sickness and death every day becomes incredibly draining.

9.1 Even as masks come off in the US in March 2022, Covid hotspots still exist around the world and new variants continue to emerge. No one knows if masks are going to be part of our lives, off and on, forever. Making commercials that show happy smiling mask-less faces might create negative backlash if things suddenly change (again) and they might even create a public relations problem if they go against future mandates.

9.2 There's now a higher cost to the free sample. So, samples will be more likely to be given of high profit margin goods. Also, people will be less inclined to huddle around the sample station, so samples won't be as easy to give out.

9.3 Athletes and movie stars have to be paid a lot for an endorsement deal. Underpaid first responders, not so much.

9.4 The focus in this question is 2022; after, hopefully, the worst of Covid has passed. The obvious con is, still, looking like your company isn't taking Covid, its risks, and its toll seriously enough. The pro is a return to normalcy. Portraying a sense that life goes on and we can smile, perchance even laugh again. Two interesting notes on this front. First, the biggest day in TV advertising (and most expensive) in the US is the Super Bowl football championship. The vast majority of this year's commercials were humorous. Second, the authors of this book had to make this decision in choosing the tone for this book. We chose to be more lighthearted. We felt this generation of students had dealt with enough.

9.5 While streaming services did increase their subscriber base during the lockdowns and work-from-home experiences, cable and satellite television still represents the vast majority of households. Add to that the fact that movie theaters and other entertainment venues were closed and there were a lot of people, suddenly watching TV. So Covid probably, and temporarily, slowed to transition of marketing dollars away from traditional media.

10.1 Never say never … some have re-opened in Buffet-ville USA, Las Vegas … but the model has a lot of problems in a world where communicable disease is a problem. Buffets only work if they have a lot of customers all the time. So, while we're hoping they do come back, it might take a while.

10.2 A lot of diagnostics comes from blood tests and that's harder to do at home. Harder, but not impossible. What are called "continuous glucose monitoring" devices have a way to monitor blood sugar levels. If that technology can be applied to other tests, many more things can be diagnosed at home.

10.3 Part of the Great Resignation was a belief that there were new employment alternatives available with a new, possibly better work–life balance. It will take time to discover whether there are such alternatives for the many people who are now looking or is this the case of "the grass is always greener"?

10.4 Aside from the obvious, the big loss will be large number of children not coming to the movies and the lost ticket sales and concession sales. The only thing that the movie theater can still be for families is an event. But again, that would certainly be a smaller number of movie theater trips overall.

10.5 Class discussion.

Index